What Must I Do To Be Saved?

The Great Awakening in Colonial America

J. M. BUMSTED
JOHN E. VAN DE WETERING

The Dryden Press
901 North Elm Street
Hinsdale, Illinois 60521

For Maxine and Ros

Copyright © 1976 by The Dryden Press
A division of Holt, Rinehart and Winston, Inc.
All rights reserved
Library of Congress Catalog Card Number: 74-25535
ISBN: 0-03-086651-0
Printed in the United States of America
6789 065 987654321

Preface

This book represents an attempt to produce a general account of an important phenomenon in colonial America. The religious revival usually known as the "Great Awakening" has been studied from many vantage points since its occurrence, and scholarly interest in it has markedly increased in recent years. Most modern literature, nevertheless, has been limited in scope and largely confined to particular regions or aspects. The aim here has been to synthesize the many modern studies and insights about the Great Awakening into a single, coherent account. Although the work lacks formal documentation, it relies heavily on the writings of many scholars and on the research—much of it unpublished—of its authors.

Because of the fragmented nature of scholarship on the revival, there is no dominant interpretation (or even interpretations) of the Great Awakening. Consequently, this book is not "revisionistic" in a general sense. To some extent we implicitly disagree with the generalizations of other students of the movement, but for the most part we can only be grateful for their findings and arguments, as the bibliography demonstrates.

Several problems, limitations, and emphases should, however, be noted in advance. The most important problem, of course, is definition. What exactly was the Great Awakening? When did it begin and when did it end? As is the case with all historical phenomena which sprawl across time and space without neat limits, the matter of dimensions is important. As the succeeding pages should make abundantly clear, the Great Awakening began in the late seventeenth century, and revivals have continued in America ever since.

We have accepted this fluidity in a large measure, but with certain conditions. One is that we have not attempted to look at American revivalism beyond the colonial period. More importantly, we have attempted to emphasize the colonial American's own view of the Great Awakening's extent. Contemporaries typically saw it as a surge of evangelical pietism in the early 1740s, and as most pronounced in those colonies to the north of Virginia. Accepting this view, we have considered the period 1740 to 1745 as the years of the Great Awakening proper, the central core of the phenomenon.

One of the results of observing contemporary usage in defining the Great Awakening is that the Southern colonies tend to be slighted in this book, as they have been generally in the literature. We are conscious of the anomalies which result: an important region gets less attention in what is described as a national movement, and that region is perhaps the one which has, in the long run, been most affected by the revivalistic impulses herein described. Nevertheless, short of writing a general history of American revivalism, the decision to follow contemporary usage seems the only way to manage the topic.

Colonial Americans thought of the events of the years 1740 to 1745 as great and general, even though the South was not equally involved in them, and while this perception may unfairly slight the Southern colonies, it is inescapable. The South is an important region in any history of American revivalism, but it was not a major area in the Great Awakening.

Another matter which ought to be mentioned is relevance. If we have attempted to be synthetic, we have also tried to be relevant—to explain the Awakening in terms understandable to the modern reader. Eighteenth-century revivalism is probably more comprehensible today than it has been for a hundred years. For most of the present century, the concerns and values of the religious pietist have been alien to the experiences of many Americans, especially those on college campuses. For the liberal intellectual, whose style of thinking has long been dominant in the academies, the intensely emotional quest of the pietist for personal salvation and moral truth could only be distasteful. Reasonable men worked together, without emotion, to build a better and more progressive world for all, but the unrest and violence of the past few years have called this ideal into serious question. Moreover, the debates on most campuses over the directions and goals of modern society have more than one direct parallel with the debates of colonial Americans over the Great Awakening. We are acutely conscious of these parallels, and we have not sought to evade their implications.

We hope readers will recognize some of the connections which we ourselves sense between our age and that of the mid-eighteenth century. At the same time, we have not sought to be overly obtrusive in relating the present to the past, since we do not seek simply to produce a tract for our own times. We have emphasized some of the resonances which we think are particularly appropriate, but on the whole we leave the reader to make his own connections and draw his own conclusions.

Finally, it is only fair to add that we, as authors, are not uncommitted in our approach to the Great Awakening. Having a sense of parallelism, we have also developed identifications and sympathies. We are, for example, far more appreciative of the pietists than were the scholars of a generation ago. Indeed, we are, as a result of our own experiences, more sympathetic to the radical and extremist wing among the revivalists than are most of those whose research we have employed. A willingness to disrupt the existing social order, which some radical New Lights displayed—in the name of a higher morality—no longer seems entirely inappropriate.

Adequate thanks for assistance in a project of this sort are impossible to extend to everyone deserving of them. In general, we are indebted to a number of scholars for their writings and continuing advice on the meaning of the Great Awakening; to a large extent this debt is recognized in the bibliography. And several generations of students have sharpened both our perceptions of the revival and the meaning of popular movements of protest.

Special thanks must go to Michael and Anita Fellman and to Ian Mugridge, all of Simon Fraser University, who read large chunks of an early draft of the manuscript and offered much constructive advice. Mike Zuckerman of the University of Pennsylvania is a friend beyond acknowledgment, not only reading an earlier draft of the manuscript with great care but offering extended criticism and support of enormous value. Robert Burke of the University of Washington has extended his usual capable editorial assistance to the project.

The Faculty Research Fund of Simon Fraser University and the History Department of the University of Montana have provided financial resources for typing the several drafts of the manuscript. Randi Johl of Simon Fraser and Sue Rabold of the University of Montana did the actual typing.

We have thanked our wives in the only possible way—by dedicating this book to them.

John E. Van de Wetering
J. M. Bumsted

Contents

Introduction

Repent, repent O Land
why will you stand it out,
Against the great eternal GOD,
till he shall drive you out.

Of all your fine possessions
which he to you hath given
And leave you not a Name nor Son
Under the Copes of Heaven.

And give your land as once
he did that of Isr'el
to Strangers and to Foreigners
to take, possess and dwell.

To Earthquakes and to Plagues
to Pestilence and War,
till for your vile transgressions
you all consumed are.

"Earnest Expostulation in the Name of the great and
glorious GOD with the Inhabitants of This Land
especially the Rising Generation," Boston, 1739

On the Lord's Day, May 7, 1738, a small convoy sailed into the harbor of Savannah Town in the frontier colony of Georgia. For many of the voyagers it had been an exceptionally long crossing, and their weeks at sea aboard the *Whitaker* had been dominated by a young clergyman sent to the wilderness as the spiritual leader of the philanthropic and pious proprietors of Georgia.

The eighteenth century had produced a new wave of humanitarianism. Man was again his brother's keeper. Above all, the soul of one's neighbor deserved attention. Thus George Whitefield had been sent to this isolated Southern frontier community to arouse concern in the settlers for the state of their souls. He remained in Georgia on this first visit only long enough to establish the roots that would make it his evangelical headquarters for several decades. Then, at the end of 1738, Whitefield returned to England to receive his formal ordination as an Anglican cleric. He was twenty-two.

In 1739, as Whitefield's time for return to the colonies approached, he toured the mother country, preaching to enormous crowds. Each sermon received unusual attention in the press. American newspapers from South Carolina to Boston picked up reports of the enthusiastic receptions and angry criticisms which accompanied Whitefield's travels. The colonies had already experienced some locally generated evangelical outbursts, suggesting a new sense of spiritual concern among many Americans. Whitefield seemed to fit the spirit of these religious awakenings and to have the nearly universal appeal that could arouse an entire community to turn to God. The colonists read of Whitefield's new personal religion in the same press that brought them frightening accounts of growing international tensions and new smallpox epidemics. Whitefield was a more hopeful item of news.

The American colonies which George Whitefield was preparing to revisit were seething with secular tensions and exulting in the excitement of conquering a wilderness. International conflict, local economic distress, and epidemics of contagious diseases were some aspects of the darker side of a country engaged in an unparalleled expansion, both numerically and spatially. The pressures of hasty growth without planning, coupled with the problems of a new society, charged the colonial atmosphere with excitement that sought an outlet and a charismatic leader. The young Anglican would supply both.

The British North America which Whitefield would arouse consisted of a number of seaboard colonies stretching from Maine (then a part of Massachusetts) to Georgia. To the northeast were Nova Scotia and Newfoundland—British, but not yet significantly peopled by English-speaking settlers. To the south was Spanish Florida. To the north, northwest, and west lay an enormous territory claimed by the King of France, with significant settlement only in the St. Lawrence River Valley between Montreal and Quebec.

No citizen lived far from the wilderness and the primitive conditions of the frontier, for American society still clustered around pockets of settlement. The frontier had not yet assumed a western line, and a traveler reached isolation more suddenly in moving north from Boston, past the vital seaport of Salem and the village of Ipswich, than in moving west through Springfield. As one journeyed from New York City south, past the settlement of Freehold, the lonely forests of New Jersey quickly closed in.

Although careful censuses were not taken in the colonial period, the population of the colonies on the eve of the Great Awakening numbered approximately 840,000. Massachusetts and Virginia (150,000 inhabitants each) were the two largest colonies, with Pennsylvania growing very rapidly, both in the city of Philadelphia and on its western borders. But regional characteristics divided the colonies into distinctly different areas, regardless of population.

Most contemporary observers divided the British colonies into three distinct sections: New England, dominated by the province of Massachusetts Bay; the Middle Colonies, dominated by Pennsylvania; and the South, dominated by Virginia. The New England colonies—New Hampshire, Massachusetts, Connecticut, Rhode Island, and perhaps Nova Scotia—were a region of small subsistence farms and coastal maritime/commercial activity, relatively homogeneous ethnically and religiously. The Middle Colonies —New York, New Jersey, Pennsylvania, the Pennsylvania Lower Counties (now Delaware)—contained several large centers of commercial and industrial activity and a sizeable number of market farms (producing mostly grain and livestock), and were already characterized by a religio-ethnic diversity which served as the prototype for the American melting pot. The South—Virginia, Maryland, the Carolinas, Georgia—had large-scale farms (usually called plantations), based on the labor of African slaves, and smaller family farms. Both types were dominated by a staple-crop economy.

Within these broad geographical regions could be found considerable variation that frequently defies generalization. The Narragansett country of southern Rhode Island, for example, was a plantation region that raised livestock, and its metropolis —Newport—had a society based upon a substantial black population, which made the city seem more like Charleston than its close neighbor, Boston.

The religious composition of the population in the various regions was equally diverse. In New England the clergy remained overwhelmingly Congregational. Although the Church of England officially coexisted with the Puritan Congregationalists, and despite Puritan leaders' deep concern over apostasy to the episcopal persuasion, Anglicanism accounted for only a small percentage of the population. The Anglican congregations in New England were in the more cosmopolitan urban areas of Boston and New Haven, but were not made up solely of the social elite.

Hidden in the larger urban centers was a tiny scattering of Baptists, organized into a church in Boston and into several churches in more tolerant Rhode Island. Outside that small, strange colony, the Baptists served as testimony to the validity of the Toleration Act of William and Mary. Although, when compared to the seventeenth century, the solidarity of Puritan New England had been broken, the presence of other denominations was more of a threat or alarm to the old Puritan way than a significant shift in the interests of the people.

Each year the colleges of Harvard and Yale turned out a supply of young preachers to replenish old Puritan pulpits and to fill new ones. The two schools, although not strictly seminaries, sent a large proportion of their graduates into the ranks of the clergy. In the first half of the eighteenth century, over one-third of each class from Harvard and one-half from Yale moved at the end of four years to teaching posts or other temporary tasks, while they finished their studies for the master's degree. The two schools provided a rather neatly balanced supply of preachers for an expanding community. Thirty percent of the new ministers from Harvard entered careers in newly established parishes, either on the frontier or in the growing, older communities. At Yale the proportion was only slightly less. The job market for young clergy varied only slightly over the full range of colonial history, but, with a particularly rapid population expansion, it was best in the early 1730s.

An area of great denominational diversity, the Middle Colonies reflected the confusion of their seventeenth-century history, as well as the warm welcome extended to religious dissenters from Europe and the British Empire. New York still showed its Dutch origins, with large numbers of Calvinistic Dutch Reformed churches to serve its native, large, and influential Dutch population. The Calvinist population of New York expanded in the first three decades of the eighteenth century as large numbers of German Reformed arrived. At the same time, a scattering of New England Puritans, trained at Harvard and especially at Yale, moved to New York to serve the few Scots, Irish, and New Englanders who settled there. A few of them continued to function as Congregationalists, while most preached as Presbyterians (the distinction was not clear for the average parishioner, since both denominations came from the English world of dissent and had moved toward unity before the turn of the century). New York also harbored a thin sprinkling of Anglicans, who were supplemented during the first two decades of the new century by fifteen missionaries from the aggressive Society for the Propagation of the Gospel in Foreign Parts (the SPG).

New Jersey held a tiny scattering of Dutch Reformed and Congregationalists. A small group of German Lutherans had settled in the southern part of the colony before the end of the 1730s. And to the west, in Hunterdon County, some Baptists had located, to be supplemented during the next decade as the denomination flourished. But the overwhelming majority of New Jersey settlers claimed affiliation with Presbyterianism. Their strength grew as numbers of Scots-Irish flooded the colony during the eighteenth century. Scattered widely through the colony, they developed in large numbers along the fertile Raritan River Valley and in Monmouth County at Freehold.

The rapid expansion of population quickly increased the demand for clergy, and the Presbyterians of the Middle Colonies suffered from a shortage throughout the first half of the century. Naturally, the new colonists sought clergymen from home. Approximately half of those who served the expanding population before 1745 came from either Ireland or Scotland, and nearly as many moved to the New Jersey wilderness from Connecticut. Since the differences between Presbyterians and Congregationalists appeared largely technical, the new Presbyterian immigrants also turned to Yale to overcome the shortage.

In Pennsylvania, the Quaker haven which since its establishment had welcomed Christian dissidents from throughout the western world, the flood of migrants in the first half of the eighteenth century added to its religious diversity. In the first two decades, German Mennonites arrived in large numbers. Most of them established settlements of great stability to the west of Philadelphia, along the Schuylkill River and in Bucks County. In the 1730s, Moravians started to arrive, settling in the Lilly country north of Philadelphia, on the borders of New Jersey. But the largest group to come to Pennsylvania in the years before the Great Awakening was Presbyterian. The majority of its supporting clergy came from Ireland, with a significant sprinkling trained and reared in Scotland. Very few New England Congregationalists wandered so far south.

In the South, the religious climate remained predominantly Anglican for the first half of the eighteenth century. Maryland had been founded as a Roman Catholic haven, but by 1690 the dissenters had smashed the Catholic control. By 1740, although some Presbyterians and a tiny scattering of other denominations persisted, the Church of England was formally established. Quakers had settled on the Eastern Shore, having fled Virginia, and had even received a visit from their leader, George Fox, late in the seventeenth century. But the second generation of these radical dissenters, like most Marylanders, were nominally of the Church of England.

In Virginia, Anglicanism dominated church life without serious challenge until 1750. Virginia's decentralized character and the absence of a New World bishop created severe tensions for the Anglican church, despite the absence of serious external challenge. Virginians always suffered from a shortage of clergy, who had to be ordained in England. As a result, native-born clergy could gain orders only at great cost. A large percentage of Virginia's clergy was, as a result, foreign born. But in the 1730s, perhaps because of the growing strength of William and Mary College as an intellectual center, a rash of local men risked the danger of sea voyage and stood the cost of the long trip to England. Since control of the church remained in London, an impressive degree of lay power had developed in each Anglican congregation.

George Whitefield was always sensitive to local religious conditions and circumstances, though he had no intention of respecting denominational preserves. And like most foreign travelers, Whitefield was more willing to view the colonies in larger terms than were the colonials themselves. For most British North Americans, it was neither a province nor a region that captured their loyalties and engaged their attentions but their local community, which provided the dominant political and social framework within which they lived, thought, and acted.

CHAPTER ONE

Communities and Tensions

On the 18th day of November last [1740], a most dreadful fire broke out in Charles-Town, and . . . this most severe and terrible calamity has succeeded the great expence the province sustained in providing for the publick defence, in the year 1737, against the impending danger of an invasion from the Spaniards; which was soon followed by the small-pox, that raged in Charles-Town during the whole year 1738, and swept off a great number of the inhabitants; and by the loss of many more by a malignant fever in the autumn of the year 1739; and after the great charge, and increase of heavy taxes, occasioned by the unsuccessful attempt which this province engaged in against St. Augustine . . . .

—From a petition of South Carolina to the House of Commons, 1740

The Great Awakening was a great outpouring of emotional energy, which took place within two contexts of critical importance. One was the local community, which provided the essential arena for an individual's life and loyalties. The other was the general atmosphere of war, death, and economic difficulties, which transcended particular communities. Each of these provided tensions and anxieties which revivalism could release and relieve.

Basically, early America contained three types of communities: coastal cities, rural agricultural communities of settled and established nature, and frontier settlements. Although the lines separating one type of community from another were not hard and fast, each community tended to produce its own social characteristics and dominant life styles, and each contained factors which would make those living there responsive to the message of spiritual regeneration preached by evangelists like George Whitefield.

The City

Cities in early America were considerably more important than their size, number, and percentage of the total population would indicate. Less than 10 percent of the American population lived in organized places with a population of more than 2,000, and the major colonial cities approximated what we would now consider a market town. Despite their small scale by modern standards, urban concentrations were the centers of political, cultural, and economic activities in the colonies. Cities like Boston (population 16,000), New York (11,000), Philadelphia (13,000), and Charleston (6,800) served as metropolitan centers for enormous hinterlands of agrarian communities and frontier settlements.

By the 1730s—on the eve of the Awakening—such clusters of population gave the colonies a new sophistication. City life assured its residents the diversities that came with the commercial bustle of prosperous seaports. Shops crowded with imported goods and well-paid local artisans producing the luxuries for a stratified, reasonably mature society were the mark of the cities. The wharves were lined by ships carrying on trade with the mother country and other colonies; the streets gathered a diverse population of crews, citizens, and immigrants.

Social homogeneity was naturally much less in urban centers than in other types of American communities, and the tensions and conflicts inherent in complex socio-economic situations were far more evident. Indeed, because cities were the publishing capitals, their problems always received much more attention in print. By the 1730s, each major town could boast a weekly newspaper which reported the prevailing political and intellectual moods to the community. No literate citizen of the New World was far removed from the tensions and fears inherent in press accounts of international crisis, for "foreign" news and news of the Empire headed each edition. As the '30s closed, the British crisis with France and Spain built to a new war, and colonists reading of it worried about the security of their coastlines.

The press offered a critical focus for events and ideas. Concern over colonial political rights gained new, broad attention through the newspapers, as details of each battle spread throughout the colonies in a largely partisan press. Governor Jonathan Belcher of Massachusetts struggled with his assembly in 1739 to gain a permanent salary grant, and colonists everywhere could follow the events. In Pennsylvania, at about the same time, the pressure of inflation and the need for paper money dominated the assembly. The papers also provided a new and popular vehicle for the prevailing intellectual moods. In the past, popular conceptions of the thinking of the intelligentsia had depended upon a trained clergy in the pulpit. Now ideas could be spread more widely and from a secular viewpoint.

In a variety of ways the city was set apart from the bulk of society in British North America, and many of its distinctive characteristics tended to make it readily susceptible to and receptive of cathartic issues and movements. A generation after the Great Awakening, the cities would take the lead in opposition to British imperial policy for many of the same reasons which made them responsive to religious revivalism at the time of George Whitefield.

Because early American cities were the commercial centers for large regions, their economic sophistication naturally meant a much more clearly and fully articulated class structure than was common in non-urban areas. Indeed, only the cities had a real class structure in the modern sense, for in frontier and rural America class distinctions were less important than status differences, which were based on other factors. Both in terms of differentials of wealth and economic activity, the cities contained a wide spectrum of classes, which was much closer to contemporary European patterns of society than was typically the case outside the metropolitan areas.

Since the cities were almost without exception provincial political capitals, the upper classes included not only ostentatiously wealthy and successful merchants but the political elite (both local and imperial) as well. At least the governor was usually a member of the British ruling class. Each city also contained a sizeable middle class, composed of professional men such as doctors, lawyers, and clergymen and including skilled artisans and shopkeepers. And each urban center had its lower classes: apprentices, indentured servants, propertyless mariners and laborers, the unemployed (mostly old or infirm), and Negro slaves. The percentage of blacks in the population varied from city to city; it was low in Boston and Philadelphia, relatively high in Newport and New York, and substantial in Charleston and Williamsburg.

Many members of the lower orders were single young men who, though they lacked much of a stake in society, could entertain hopes of acquiring one. However, a fair proportion of the lower class, including the permanently unfree Negro, represented an exploited and oppressed group that was accustomed to hardship and violence. The city had a population which could mobilize at any time into that relatively formless aggregation known as "the mob," and few cities in the colonies were free from at least occasional outbursts of mob activity and violence. It is not always clear from contemporary sources whether the mobs of early America were composed of the urban poor, but they had enormous popular support. A Boston clergyman observed in 1737:

A great and new affliction has befallen, even shameful and vile disorders at Boston, murmuring against the Government and the rich people among us as if they could (by any means within their Power, besides Prayer) have prevented the rise of provisions. A number of five or six hundred men rose one night and pulled down the Market Place and the Town have been so wroth as to vote the disposing of the places to other uses, . . . and none of the Rioters or Mutineers have been yet discovered or if suspected seem to regard it, their favourers being so many.

But if the urban populace could become a mob, it could also emerge as an audience or crowd, to which revivalists like George Whitefield could preach with visible impact. Indeed, the clergyman himself suggests part of the relationship.

The very characteristics of those composing the lower orders of urban American society made them receptive to the type of spontaneous, emotional, and visible religious experience which the revivalists encouraged. Not only were they individuals without social standing, they were also frequently newcomers to the urban environment, either recent immigrants from overseas (most of whom landed and remained in the major urban seaports) or migrants from the back country. They suffered more from hardships of climate and economic fluctuations than did their country cousins, and food shortages could be disastrous. As the events of 1737 in Boston indicate, the urban poor were becoming accustomed to venting their frustrations through action, through the emotional responses of crowd activity. Public catharsis could provide solace for a hard lot in life.

In an age which still held church membership and religious experience as important and meaningful social values, the upwardly mobile among the urban poor (as well as their middle-class brethren) could seek a spiritual regeneration, which provided some measure of personal security and satisfaction, some place in society and life. And many ministers and members of the ruling group undoubtedly saw revival as a potential alternative to other forms of violence, at least at the beginning. The urban audience for evangelists like Whitefield could hardly be confined to the lower orders; all classes were represented within the crowd. But contemporary descriptions make it quite clear that the bottom layer of urban society composed a large proportion of the substantial crowds which flocked to hear the great itinerant preachers of the Awakening.

The city thus provided a potential audience for the revivalists. It also provided the means of publicizing and recording the excitement of a mass movement, and a forum for discussing the issues engendered by one. Newspapers, book publishers, the pulpits of influential clergymen, coffee houses and taverns all represented highly concentrated media which not only disseminated the news of the day but, to a large extent, created and shaped it as well. The urban media were responsible for giving form to the scattered threads of emotional religious outbursts in the colonies, which turned them into a recognizable movement. Once the cities had experienced the "great and glorious" revival of religion, once the intellectuals and the opinion makers concentrated in the urban areas perceived the importance of what was happening, its extension and expansion was made much easier. Country folk were drawn to the city from the hinterland to see for themselves what they were hearing and reading about. Even those in the back country who could not visit the city could learn of the great events from newspapers, pamphlets, and eyewitnesses.

Finally, a spirit of relative denominational openness and toleration, found in most early American cities, made it possible for itinerant evangelists to make an ecumenical appeal. No city in colonial America was more tolerant than Philadelphia, where Quakers, Presbyterians, Baptists, Anglicans, and a variety of German sects had long flourished and contended with one another. But in all cities the audiences for evangelists were readily available, the means of recruiting them accessible, and few obstacles existed—either overt or covert—to the gathering of a crowd in the open air to hear a series of sermons by nonresident preachers. Among the competing religious groups, the visitor could anticipate finding one or more receptive to his presence, and could expect some intellectual backing as well.

The city was the obvious place to publicize the principles of itinerant evangelicalism. Once they had been established, it was much easier to extend them into an inherently less receptive countryside. Urban conditions have always been more conducive to new fashions and have provided models for the countryside to follow. The ready availability of crowds, the media, the absence of constraints on the activities of strangers—these were inducements to revivalism unique to the city.

The Settled Agrarian Community

Thomas Prince, a leading Boston minister, commented about Massachusetts in 1730: "Give me leave to observe, That tho' the Principal Sea-Port Towns of the Province are exceedingly exposed and deprav'd by the Pouring in of Trade and Strangers, yet we may by no means judge by These the Rest of the Countrey." Prince's observations held true for the colonies in general. Unlike the cities, where the dominant style was openness, complexity, and conflict, the agrarian communities of early America emphasized the stable values of order and relative uniformity. Despite the obvious importance of the city and the romantic myths which have grown up about the frontier, most Americans in 1740 lived in reasonably well established agrarian communities.

The political structures of agrarian communities varied considerably, from the village or town-meeting democracies of New England to the spatially scattered plantation county oligarchies of much of the South. Basic economic structures tended to vary as well. Although most of the small farmers and planters of early America are usually described as "subsistence" farmers (producing the essentials of life on the individual farm unit), no farmer was totally independent of the market and external sources of production. Many small farmers and planters engaged in other activities, such as fishing, trapping, or artisan manufacturing, at least for part of the year. Most of them also grew some sort of cash crop for at least a local market. Large-scale farmers in the Middle Colonies and the great planters of the South were dependent upon outside markets, and they struggled as desperately for self-sufficiency as did the small producers who worked to grow a salable crop. The life style of a Virginia planter who traded with London merchants was obviously quite different from that of a small dirt farmer. Nonetheless, in terms of social homogeneity and ideal stability, agrarian communities throughout the colonies had a good deal in common.

Most rural Americans in the eighteenth century tied their lives to the natural rhythms of the day and the seasons. They rose with the sun and went to bed at dusk. Although daylight was shorter in winter, they had more leisure at this time of year. From spring to autumn, from planting to harvesting, the entire family was engaged in activities related to agriculture. Events in their lives, from private ones such as marriage and the birth of children to public ones such as political, military, and religious obligations, were conditioned by the pressures or absence of pressure of the growing season. British army officers discovered (to their dismay) how difficult it was to keep colonial farmers in camp at harvest time.

From New Hampshire to the South, whether the farming unit was a few acres of rocky pasturage or hundreds of fertile acres of tobacco plantation, the colonial American was sensitive to the vagaries of nature. Disasters like droughts and earthquakes were much more than natural events in such a world. They were, instead, blows that stunned men's confidence in the harmony of their lives—direct interference with nature by the hand of God. The need for explanation and reassurance was powerful, and could easily be exploited by the revivalist.

The identity with nature which everyone shared, combined with the relatively unsophisticated nature of economic life in every agrarian community, eliminated the visible class divisions of the city. Not all individuals, of course, were perfectly equal, but distinctions were of "status"—rather than "class" in the modern sense. Inequality was frequently a subtle characteristic of agrarian society. Wealth, especially landed wealth, was a factor, but perhaps equally important were less obvious factors such as age and family connections.

In many communities the important distinction was between the mature family householders and the young. Settled communities, especially outside the South, placed no particular premium on youth. An individual was usually over thirty before he gained recognition as a full-fledged member of the community. While deep class divisions were not the cause of revivalism in such places, the rural young were susceptible to a movement which offered them some entry into adult society. Church membership was frequently taken as a mark of maturity.

Society in the South was somewhat different. The basic social divisions among the white population were between leaders and followers, and the leadership did not always come from a clearly definable upper stratum. Nevertheless, white unity was based upon exploitation of the Negro slave, who formed an obvious bottom rung for society. The blacks, who formed a target for revivalistic activities everywhere in the colonies, were far more numerous in the South. Moreover, slave labor and a market-farming economy based upon large amounts of land—the fundamental component of wealth in agrarian America—made possible the emergence of a group of self-conscious and recognized landed gentlemen. As the Virginia minister, Devereux Jarrett, said of his colony in the 1730s:

> We were accustomed to look upon what were called gentle folks as being of a superior order. For my part, I was quite shy of them and kept off at an humble distance. A periwig in those days was a distinguished badge of gentle folk, and when I saw a man riding the road near our house with a wig on, it would so alarm my fears and give me such a disagreeable feeling that I dare say I would run off, as for my life. Such ideas of the difference between "gentle" and "simple" were, I believe, universal among all of my rank and age.

The major planter families were almost totally immune to the call of revivalism, but the social distance they kept from "simple folk" prevented their distaste for the revival from influencing the bulk of the population. Indeed, many planters came to associate revivalism with a form of religion that was quite proper for the lower orders, and were quite prepared to condone its extension among them as an element of social control.

Unlike the cities, which contained churches of many denominations and offered a fair degree of religious choice to urban residents—whether or not they took advantage of it—agrarian communities were usually served by a single church before the

Great Awakening. In part, this was a practical matter. A small population in a New England village or a Virginia county was seldom financially equipped to support multiple religious institutions. But in larger measure the key reason for the single church was the sense most inhabitants retained that their church was an integral part of the community. In New England, the community church was usually Congregational Puritan; in the Middle Colonies it was German or Dutch Reformed, Lutheran, Presbyterian, or Quaker; in the South it was Anglican.

The church was part of an individual's life from birth and baptism through marriage to death, and it performed other social functions as well. Attendance at worship service was a social occasion for young and old alike, and most churches offered themselves (those in New England with much insistence) as arbiters in the affairs of the community. The emphasis, by and large, was on the value of the sacraments rather than on the quality of the individual's religious experience. Most Americans did not want to abandon the sacraments, but many sought a vital religious experience as well.

Criteria for church membership varied from denomination to denomination and local church to local church, but by 1740 church membership in most agrarian communities—to the minds of the inhabitants—should have been synonymous with community residence. In New England, the ministry never tired of stressing the united community which had existed in the seventeenth century and had gradually been lost. Southern Anglicans still retained the older British notion of "One Church, One State." Most colonials were thus prepared to hold that church membership provided a sense both of self-identity and community identification. The young, whose need for both identifications were greatest, were thus particularly susceptible to any religious experience which could provide this need.

Another important aspect of the church pertained to those who felt geographically isolated from it. Even within the coastal plain region of greatest population and predominantly stable communities, some lived on the outskirts of settlement. Psychological perceptions of distance varied from region to region and time to time. In New England, four or five miles seemed to many in outlying areas too far to live from church; in the South, twenty miles or more might be acceptable. But in all regions the tolerable distance was lessening as the population grew and expanded. If the church building was too far, then it would somehow have to be brought closer, since few were willing to surrender access to religious services. For those living on the fringes of a community, revivalism offered a way to accomplish this, to have a more accessible community church.

Stability, order, harmony—these were the important values to agrarian communities, since inhabitants lived in close proximity to one another both in their houses and in their communities. The South may never have developed a viable village society, and even in New England most villages had rapidly broken down into scattered individual farmsteads. But living patterns within the dwelling unit in all regions stressed cooperation and togetherness. The notion of a space within the house as the private sanctum of one individual member of a family was virtually unknown except among the upper classes. Child-rearing practices emphasized discipline and avoided tendencies toward personal conflict by not inculcating the values of individuality and privacy.

Outside the home, the institutions of both church and government reinforced family values. Disagreement and disunity were distasteful to the community. While it is tempting to use some modern psychological term such as "repressed" to describe colonial agrarian society, the term requires some adjustment to the values of the eighteenth century. The members of both the family and the community had no perception of constraint. Moreover, certain approved outlets, such as legal litigations provided a release of hostilities. All observers of colonial America were struck by the readiness of Americans to go to law, frequently over minor matters. Litigation, therefore, was less an evidence of the value of social conflict than of its disapproval.

In such a society, violence and conflict were not so much acceptable values as necessary, if unrecognized, outlets for release of tension. Quite unconsciously, many Americans wanted and needed acceptable ways of releasing the tensions resulting from the uncertainties of their lives and of expressing their emotions. Few ways were potentially more acceptable than religion. Religious revival clearly offered another safety valve in an ordered community.

The Frontier

The frontier provided another type of community in eighteenth-century America, with its own particular receptivity to revival. Few back-country communities were settled by the familiar seventeenth-century process of transplanting whole villages, complete with minister and social order. A back-country settlement was typically composed of relative strangers, united mainly by the common experience of having uprooted themselves from their familiar surroundings—either in Europe or America—and faced with the need to begin life anew, in both a personal and an institutional sense. The very act of moving to the back country suggests a personality rather more innovative and individualistic than the bulk of the population that was left behind in settled communities, although it is impossible to say how many were forced to migrate by poverty and the absence of available land in settled communities. Nevertheless, new opportunities—economic, social, and personal—offered the principal motive for risking the unknown.

Frontier communities were in the process of becoming. Each settler on the frontier faced new, strange, and frightening demands for adaptation to new surroundings and conditions. Some perennial pioneers in colonial America moved restlessly from wilderness area to wilderness area in search of a satisfaction they never found. But most back-country settlers came from established agrarian communities in either America or Europe, and found themselves face to face with an instability that had not been a part of their experience.

The frontier offered an opportunity for innovation, and change from previous patterns was possible. But most settlers, while intellectually prepared to be different, emotionally craved the reassurance of the familiar. Hence back country people moved as quickly as possible to replicate institutions with which they were comfortable. The back-country experience produced a rough egalitarianism, since every man's problems were more or less the same, but the conditions of equality were acted out within the framework of the traditional. Settlers, whether New England Yankees or German sectarians, attempted as best they could to re-create the conditions and institutions of their previous life. For the most part, settlers created patterns of land allocation and political control which suited their experiences and their needs, whatever the external government might demand.

The resolution of conflicting experiences and tensions with central government did not necessarily provide amenities. This was particularly true with one of the most important institutions of most settlers' previous existence: the church. Before 1740, religion in America had not adapted itself to the demands of the moving frontier. The churches of the colonies were organized in European fashion, in terms of stable communities, either urban or agrarian. For most settlers, a church meant a building and an incumbent clergyman attached to the edifice. Both building and clergyman had to be paid for out of funds which, most individuals and the community could agree, were more needed elsewhere. A decent roof over one's head, a sufficient amount of cleared land, fences, and roads—all these had priority over the erection of a church building and the hiring of a minister.

The pioneer recognized postponement of the satisfaction of his spiritual needs as one of the prices of beginning again. Before the Great Awakening he did not question any of the assumptions upon which deferral was based. Ministers expected to be paid, and if there was no money, obtaining a clergyman must wait. Although back-country settlements were hardly free of disagreement and conflict, such conditions were probably less important in explaining the frontier's eager response to revivalism than the simple absence of organized religion. Even before 1740, the practice of employing one clergyman for more than one parish was common in large parts of the back country. Such a minister would travel from one parish to another on a regular schedule, spending a few weeks in each place. Really a system of distributing available resources within a traditional context, it was considerably different from the itinerancy introduced by the revival, and contemporaries recognized the distinction.

The Great Awakening provided both clergymen and settlers

with new assumptions, including financial ones, which made it possible for all parts of the back country to acquire some measure of a formal religious experience. The fact that the experience was emotionally satisfying to the frontiersman was incidental, although certainly helpful.

Colonial Tensions

To this point we have been emphasizing the spiritual and emotional needs of the American population in terms of communities. But colonists on the eve of the Great Awakening also had needs which transcended the type of community in which they resided. Every society faces constant threats and problems, and certainly those faced by Americans in the 1730s were little different from the ones they confronted throughout the eighteenth century. Nevertheless, forebodings of war, economic crisis, epidemic disease, and ethnic tensions created a continual uneasiness which could lead to a cathartic emotional experience such as the Great Awakening.

Despite the general peace which followed the Treaty of Utrecht in 1713, North American frontiers continued to be scenes of frequent outbursts of violence involving colonists (British, French, and Spanish) and their Indian allies. The Carolina frontier and northern Massachusetts were particularly active arenas of bloodshed, especially in the 1720s. Although open warfare was minimal throughout most of the 1730s, the fear of a resumption of fighting was always present. War was a constant concern to colonials on the exposed limits of settlement and, perhaps more important, tended to constrain Americans in established regions from moving to areas where land was more plentiful and available.

The continuing back-country hostilities became war in October 1739, when Britain declared war on Spain. Even before the outbreak of open fighting, the high seas, like the frontier, had become dangerous territory. Writing of the year 1739, Josiah Cotton of Plymouth hoped that American mariners "were more grateful of their gracious preserver from the danger of the Seas & enemies," noting that "the Spaniards have taken many of the English vessells this year."

Word of the British declaration of war reached the colonies in

November 1739, at precisely the same time that George Whitefield arrived to begin his preaching tour. The British quickly began recruiting in the colonies for a major land and sea expedition against Cartegena in Cuba, and sought 3,500 colonials to compose an American regiment. As enlistments mounted, many Americans became increasingly concerned about the possibility of the entry of France into the war. Spain and France were familiar mutual allies, and France was British America's traditional enemy. A French involvement would unleash thousands of hostile Indians along the British frontier, from Nova Scotia to Virginia. Fear of the French received no immediate resolution, since the war with France did not actually begin until 1744.

Many disturbing economic difficulties also faced British North America in the 1730s. One problem was an unfavorable balance of trade, which drained America of gold and silver, creating a continual shortage of a medium of exchange. The solution to this endemic difficulty in the early eighteenth century was the issuance of paper money by many colonies, usually in the form of bills of credit anticipating provincial tax revenue.

A newer problem was an increasing shortage of readily available and inexpensive land in the seacoast regions of stable settlements. A letter published in 1738 by Pennsylvania German settlers complained that

> because of the number of people who have immigrated and the increase in population, the good land has become so rare that it is to be considered good fortune when someone finds a good piece of land with all of the necessities provided, for which, accordingly, he must pay a high enough price even if it is far from Philadelphia, the only large city in the country.

The situation was worse in other, less well endowed regions than Pennsylvania, particularly in New England.

The shortages of money (and credit) and land were connected by many colonials, resulting in a series of proposals in several colonies for currency emissions based upon land security: the "land banks." New England, and especially Massachusetts, was the center of the great controversy over such credit schemes in the

1730s. Arguments in favor of the land banks stressed the opportunity afforded by such credit to obtain and improve new land.

In Massachusetts the debate produced a charge from the Boston town meeting that land bank opponents reduced the townsfolk to "have our Bread & Water measured out to Us by those who Riot in Luxury & Wantonness on Our Sweat & Toil and be told by them that we are too happy, because we are not reduced to Eat Grass with the Cattle," and an accusation from the countryside that Boston merchants were "Enemies to the Country." While such charges might have been rhetorical exaggerations, the land bank controversy, of which they were a part, produced a political crisis in Massachusetts which also coincided almost exactly with George Whitefield's arrival in the colony.

In Pennsylvania, a paper currency was managed with less conflict. Nevertheless, the winter of 1740/41 saw a lack of small change in Philadelphia and attempts to provide substitutes, which merchants refused to accept. The result was several nights of mob activity.

Like war and economic difficulties, pestilence and plague were not unfamiliar threats to Americans. The colonists recognized that at any time their communities could be devastated by epidemic disease for which there were few preventatives and no cures. Although some control had been attained over the dreaded smallpox, it was achieved only by the dangerous practice of inoculation with weakened strains of the disease itself. Given a general medical helplessness in the face of contagious and frequently fatal disease, it is hardly surprising that the colonials sought reassurance in the eternal promises of religion whenever they were faced with reports about or the presence of dreaded and often unfamiliar epidemic diseases, especially those which threatened the young. Most saw such adversities as judgments of God for individual and corporate sin.

New England and New York were struck in the mid-1730s by a particularly virulent outbreak of diphtheria and scarlet fever, which not only proved fatal for many but also may have weakened children and encouraged susceptibility to other diseases. Certainly an epidemic of measles in the Northeastern colonies from 1739 to 1741 carried off larger numbers of the population than was typically the case with this relatively innocuous disease. The measles situation was so serious in the Boston area in 1739 that the Harvard commencement was canceled. In the South, Virginia experienced a yellow fever epidemic at the end of the 1730s, and the first major outbreak of whooping cough in America struck South Carolina in 1738.

Establishing a direct correlation between contagious diseases and revivalism has not proved possible. But, at the very least, the outbreaks of epidemics of the 1730s contributed to a general concern over the uncertain nature of existence in the colonies. And many colonials could but agree with Josiah Cotton when he wrote that "the Diseases of our bodies proceed from the distempers of our minds some of which diseases the nature and constitutions of men admits but one of the life of man."

Outbreaks of mob violence and public disorder in the major cities at the turn of the 1740s were symptomatic of the high level of discontent endured by Americans. Each city had its particular difficulties, but each responded with disorder and repression. Between 1730 and 1740, for example, orders for ships in Boston yards dropped from forty to twenty a year. There was a corresponding 66 percent decline in fishing, distilling, and allied trades. Boston's energy was directed into tearing down markets and then into the land bank disputes.

In New York, the decade of the 1730s was one of escalating racial tensions between the city's white population and an increasing black one, culminating in 1740 with a panic over an alleged slave plot aided by Roman Catholic priests from Canada. In Philadelphia, the mob was on the streets in the winter of 1740/41, and the eve of an election in 1742 saw a street battle between sailors and armed Germans and Quakers.

In South Carolina, an area not far from Charleston was struck in 1739 by an abortive but nonetheless violent slave uprising. Concern spilled over into the city, for this was the first eruption in the South involving large numbers of blacks. The city also experienced a serious fire that same year. Charleston merchant Robert Pringle wrote that the fire "came so suddenly upon us as well as the great Risque we Run from an Insurrection of our Negroes which we were very apprehensive of, but all as yet Quiet by the street Guards & watch we are oblig'd to keep Constantly night & Day.''

While a similar catalogue of troubles could be made for the colonies in any decade, not every period brought to the omnipresent tensions both an intellectual position and individuals capable of fusing tensions and ideas in a single movement. Such a fusion of ideas, tensions, and men occurred twice in America in the colonial period. In 1775 it produced the American Revolution; a generation earlier it had spawned the Great Awakening.

Psychologically, colonial Americans were probably always ready for emotional catharsis. But to understand the coming of revivalism as a general movement, we must turn to the men and the ideas.

CHAPTER TWO

European Challenges to Formalism

Our life is as a fire dampened, or as a fire shut up in stone. Dear children, it must blaze, and not remain smouldering, smothered. Historical faith is mouldy matter–it must be set on fire: the soul must break out of the reasoning of this world into the life of Christ, into Christ's flesh and blood; then it receives the fuel which makes it blaze. There must be seriousness; history reaches not Christ's flesh and blood.

—Jacob Boehme, *De Incarnatione Verbi*

The outburst of religious enthusiasm and pietism which struck North America with full impact in 1740 did not develop in either an intellectual or a geographical vacuum. Indeed, men like George Whitefield and Jonathan Edwards were the heirs and spokesmen of a long European tradition which had helped prepare the way for revivalism. Two concurrent intellectual developments in seventeenth- and eighteenth-century Europe were critical in preparing men and their minds for the Great Awakening. One of these was the Enlightenment, the most influential feature of which was the rise of scientific thought and investigation. The other was a new emphasis upon individual spiritual experience and emotional identity with God, a concern usually called pietism.

Science and pietism would seem at first glance to be totally contrary and irreconcilable movements, one rational, the other emotional. But as the German scholar Dietmar Rothermund has pointed out,

> Rationalism and mysticism are not contradictory approaches; they spring from the same source, the reliance on inner light and experience rather than on authority and tradition. The real contrast is rather the one between objective and subjective mysticism—the one relying on outward means like the sacraments, the other on introspection and an analysis of the experience of the soul.

Scientists and pietists could unite in opposition to a shared enemy, which was not reason arguing from experience but logic deducing from inherited first principles. The shared reaction was to the academic scholasticism which served as the accepted intellectual truth at the beginning of the seventeenth century all over Europe, to that century's version of the modern university academic, whose great wisdom extends in all directions except to what is *really* happening, either in the world or in his own heart.

Pietism in Continental Europe

Ideas have never respected international boundaries. The beginnings of the fully developed eighteenth-century pietist movement can be discovered in the religious literature and preaching of each major Protestant area: English Puritan, Reformed Calvinist, and German Lutheran. For the emerging pietists of the seventeenth century, religious experience meant an "inner sense" of understanding the truths of religion, which led to a deeply felt and often highly charged conviction resulting in "conversion." Since English Puritanism from its beginnings incorporated a strong pietist strain, English authors were translated and absorbed on the Continent at an early date. England, accordingly, had an especially strong influence on Protestant pietism.

From the Netherlands, with its Calvinist affinity for the English Puritans, a steady stream of pietist preachers traveled to England to observe and study. And in both England and the Netherlands— as well as in the New England colonies in America—the *Medulla Sacrae Theologiae* of William Ames (English by birth and training but Dutch by migration and experience) served as a basic text. Each area produced its own dedicated pietists, emphasizing faith over reason, a "rebirth" for salvation, and a special attention to the moral life. The passionate appeals of the Anglican Richard Baxter, the vernacular preaching of the Reformed Jadocus van Lodensteyn, and the pleas to the heart by the Lutheran John Arndt shared common religious concerns. Each may have belonged to a distinctive pietist movement, but the cross currents from area to area provided an international flavor.

The international movement toward "vital pietism" or spiritual and experiential revivalism found, in the eighteenth century, new and critical stimulus from the well-organized and highly successful pietist movement in Germany. German pietism had emerged from the confusion following the Thirty Years' War. It provided emotional reassurances and security for a people whose lives had been disrupted and disorganized by the devastation of a war not particularly of their making or concern.

The appeal of the German pietists to the inner mysteries of "sensual" religion could be traced in part to the mysticism of the cobbler of Gorlitz, Jacob Boehme, who emphasized Christ's dwelling within the heart, Boehme's mysticism was not the familiar rejection of the material world of the flesh in favor of self-flagellation, but an exaltation of the beauties of the body and its functions. He made little distinction between physical love and love of Christ. Boehme's insistence upon the unity of physical and spiritual love caught a human intuition that is always present, needing only proper circumstances to be liberated. Both personalism and a heightened social conscience (as with many of today's young) could find expression within a Christian tradition in a world freed of the dead hand of scholasticism. Nevertheless, Boehme's mysticism was too extreme for many pietists. Organization was always easier to emphasize than emotional sensuousness.

While Boehme stressed love, other pietists emphasized institutional reform. Philip Jacob Spener was crucial here. Spener early organized local "collegia pietatis" for Bible study, seeking to harness and focus the pietist mood. His major work, *Pia Desideria*, appeared in 1675 to set the first foundations of the German movement. Profoundly social in his concern, Spener threw religious responsibility onto the individual—where it had traditionally belonged—but he also stressed the individual's role in contemporary society. He emphasized Bible study, lay participation in church government, and the practical nature of Christianity. Instead of doctrinal refinements, he urged "practical" preaching and devotion.

Spener's successor was August Herman Francke, who transmitted the German pietistic developments to the English-speaking world. Francke arrived at the pietist University of Halle in 1691 as a refugee from religious presecution. He remained there, first as a professor of Greek and Oriental languages, then as professor of theology, until his death in 1727. Under Francke, the German pietistic movement received wide international attention, as it increasingly caught much of the spirit of the reformist humanitarianism of the early eighteenth century.

Many who were not pietists were struck by Francke's approaches to reform. Indeed, this was pietism's strength. It was not a denomination, not a theological school, but a posture and attitude. Typically, the German pietist reformers emphasized a return to primitive Christianity and interdenominationalism. The Christian world, they said, had been divided into warring sects, much as Germany had been in the mid-seventeenth century. But most of the conflict occurred over mere "notions, which rather swell the fancy with a set of nice and subtle distinctions" and fail to "afford any wholesome food to the soul." Feeding the soul transcended doctrinal differences.

German pietists like Francke were primarily concerned with saving souls, but they stressed in particular the neglected souls of the poor and uneducated. In fact, the German reformers showed a concern for education which belied their overt antiintellectualism:

> Many boys of good natural parts and endowments, by reason of which they might be made fit for great undertaking, but for want of education, lying buried under the rubbish of ignorance are now found out, and their pregnant genius . . . cultivated, and polish'd for the common benefit.

Although education needed to be spiritual and moral as a preparation for salvation, the pietists found ethical and spiritual values in literacy. To their minds, their schools were seminaries for the general good of the country. Education, moreover, offered a means to attack poverty, for ignorance and poverty moved together.

The simple, nonrational call of the German reformers caught hold all over Europe. In Germany, although the principal intellectual spokesmen for pietism were reformers of the German Lutheran establishment, a host of minor sects was spawned or reinvigorated in the half century after the Thirty Years' War. The Brethren, the Moravians, the Mennonites were only a few of the more important new sects. Despite differences of opinion on church organization and discipline, all emphasized the religion of the heart. Many of these groups experienced persecution on religious grounds in Europe, and since most appealed to the dislocated, persecution and dislocation combined to produce powerful motives for migration. Many found their way eventually to the New World, where Pennsylvania's rich land and promises of religious freedom were particularly attractive.

The attitudes of the pietists migrated as well. John Jennings, the successful director of an English nonconformist academy, translated Francke's chief work, *Pietas Hallensis*, which appeared in London in 1707. The German reformer, who appealed to a sense of optimism and an accompanying sense of personal dignity, offered a religion full of joy and love. The faith, dignity, and love of a Christian, wrote Francke, must be "represented in [their] most amiable and attractive light in order to win sinners to the ways of religion." Then, carefully and deliberately, he abandoned the God of fear and built his case on the benevolent God of love.

Fear, he argued, keeps man from God, for He works through the "royal law of love" as the spring of all faculties of the soul. Fear belonged to the sinner and love moved the righteous. The spring from which man's fear arose was love of the world and a want of self-denial. Francke wrote about external forces of evil fear as well, which pushed the individual along the road to sin. These social sources of fear offered Francke a chance to attack the established churches and governments. Fear, he found, followed from the tyranny of those in power. Francke then placed himself unequivocally on the side of the humble, for fear was greatest among men of "first rank," who have the most to lose.

For Francke and the pietists, for those who read their works, and for the Great Awakening generally, the love of God was the "sense" of the thing. One could feel the truth of Him once one had achieved spiritual harmony (however difficult to define) with Him. The individual needed no logic or "lifeless formality," but only an inward sense of religion. The pietists poured invective on the slaves of reason. They damned "the specious and plausible reasonings of such as follow their corrupt reason more than the word of God." Here was the focus of the pietist position. Fine theological distinctions, inherited from hundreds of years of religious disputation, meant little. Religion was of the heart, and it was found through the senses.

Francke not only offered an international call for "experiential" religion but he gave his readers a sermon style as well. Each sermon, he wrote, should be designed to bring the sinner to conversion through the use of "lively color" in the parson's speech. But his cry for passionate preaching was also directed toward an optimistic view of salvation. John Jennings, in explaining the new sermon style for English audiences, seemed to merge two strands into a single style. First, Jennings described an evangelist's emotional call as designed to arouse the passion of his listener and thus to aid in securing a change of "heart." Second, the appeal had to be useful: "Let us take the spirit and style of scriptures and thence borrow bold figures and delusions, strong descriptions and commanding address to the passions." The pietists sought a new level of participation in religion. Once aroused, one could become totally involved.

English Pietism

The reception of Francke and other pietists in England was aided by their compatability with an English movement stressing proper conduct and detailed attacks on the sins of the community. Religious reformers in times of social chaos, like the German pietists or the "Jesus Freaks" of our own day, have shown a special concern for the conduct of their supporters. The pietists required high standards of self-discipline and urged that all members of the community help one another achieve the standards of conduct of the past. The England of Queen Anne and the early Hanoverians was not quite in social chaos, but many found it corrupt and sought a reformation of manner.

One leader of this movement was Josiah Woodward, who appealed to otherwise staid and moderate clergymen of the Church of England. Although hardly a pietist, Josiah Woodward lamented the serious decline in the community's standards of conduct. He called for recovery, before the "vengeance of an angry God" fell upon the society. Echoing Puritan critics of an earlier generation, the Anglican minister cried out against the "degenerate and debauch'd" times. He portrayed a war "betwixt the Prince of Light and that of Darkness." In the face of such moral decline, he encouraged the creation of religious societies made up of young men dedicated to the improvement of the moral tone of the community. These societies, in their demand for new behavior which would aid the social salvation of the entire community, were one step short of the impassioned plans of the revivalists forty years later. Membership in such a religious society, after all, depended upon the participants' "solemn account of their sense of spiritual things."

The announced object of the organizations, as explained under pressure from the Bishop of London, was to "quicken" religious interest and preparation for the other world. As self-proclaimed moral arbiters of the community, the young reformers sought a revival of their own. To the secular community they were self-righteous snoopers who interfered with personal freedom. But the "lovers of vice" did not get far with their complaints, for the societies were merely attempting to enforce traditional laws (mainly Elizabethan in origin) governing deportment.

In 1702 Woodward wrote delightedly that the institution of the religious society had spread to Scotland, Ireland, and America. About the same time (and with enormous satisfaction), he quoted the laws of the land that suppressed bawdy and gaming houses and prevented the sale of liquor, chocolate, and coffee on the Sabbath. To spread his good works toward the reformation of manners, Woodward prepared small pamphlets on specific sins. These became extremely popular, evidently catching a mood that demanded greater attention to morality, or perhaps a general conviction of the times that man could improve his condition on earth. Whatever theological difficulties such ideas might present, they caught the fancy of a public that worried little about intellectual consistency. Woodward's pamphlets passed through many editions, and were joined by the revival of a great many older popular guides to Christian conduct. In the decades before revival, as the demand or drive for better deportment spread, as the revivalists of the past found new fame in new editions, and as the words of the German pietists reached the English public, the leading English publicists of the new spirit also found an audience.

The new posture took hold in many curious quarters. Isaac Watts, the famous hymnologist and scholar, was no pietist. Nevertheless, he declared, "Cold reason will not convert"; the most moving method of speech possible was needed in the pulpit. Intellectually, Watts was entirely comfortable with right reason: "It must be acknowledged, indeed, the honor of the present age, that we have some pretenses above our predecessors, to freedom and justice of thought, to strength of reasoning, to clear ideas." As a result of that clear, free thought, Watts implied, experiential religion must gain support and strength. Then he launched a new appeal to touch the heart.

As the works of Watts appeared and his name became known to the British public, the more powerful intellect of William Law was brought to bear on the pietist movement. Law, reared in a comfortable middle-class family and a graduate of Cambridge, had prepared for the Anglican ministry. But deep conviction led him to refuse the oath of allegiance to George II. Denied a pulpit, he became a prolific and popular author. In the traditional Puritan way, Law insisted that every act must be for the glory of God. But he soon turned to matters of personal conduct in this world and expanded the broadly felt concern for deportment, initiated by Woodward, into a firm pietist social conscience.

William Law paid traditional attention to the concept of the spiritual life, demanding pious prayer, humility, and self-denial. Then he turned his attention to society. All man's activities, he argued, must be conducted with social concern. Law's outline of proper conduct for the tradesman was typical: "He will buy and sell, labour and travel, because by so doing he can do some good to himself and others." The riches of business success that inevitably fell to a properly diligent and pious tradesman could not be displayed as extravagant material signs of wealth and pleasure. A rich man must deny himself the "pleasures and indulgences" of costly apparel. Even more specifically, Law attacked the sin of swearing. This seemingly minor breach of proper decorum was serious evidence of the neglect of religion.

A Serious Call to a Devout and Holy Life, perhaps the most influential book on religion of the early eighteenth century, was published by Law in 1729. Dr. Samuel Johnson said he first picked up *A Serious Call* expecting to find it dull, but allowing the laugh of contempt. Instead, he observed, "I found Law quite an overmatch for me; and this was the first occasion of my thinking in earnest of religion." At first, few could accept Law's argument that salvation depended upon "the sincerity and perfection of our endeavors to obtain it." But within a few years, many were acting as though they had originated the notion.

Not only Samuel Johnson but the Wesleys and George Whitefield were profoundly influenced by Law's early writings, although Law later turned to a mysticism rooted in the thought of Jacob Boehme, in which few followed him. Law's only major disciple of his Boehmistic phase was an obscure and self-taught Nova Scotia evangelist named Henry Alline. But in his earlier devotional works William Law bridged the gap for Englishmen between a simplistic drive for "proper" personal conduct and a spirit of revival. He linked questions of social deportment to the inner life as the express manifestations of the soul's godly impulses. William Law was a recluse, and it took the Wesley brothers to put into practice Law's fusion of the Woodward moral life movement with pietism.

John Wesley emphasized the disciplinary aspects of the society, forming at Oxford a little cell of those who, like himself, had responded to Law's call for Christian conduct based on a religion of the heart. Wesley's movement remained for most of the century within the Anglican church as a radical wing. His personal inclinations emphasized the achievement of spiritual regeneration through self-discipline, with—said his critics—a minimum of love and a maximum of pride. But one of those who had been attracted to Wesley at Oxford was a young man named George Whitefield, who was deeply affected by reading William Law's *A Serious Call*. The merger of pietism and moral reform within the Church of England would lead directly, through Whitefield, to the American Great Awakening.

Enlightenment Science

In the seventeenth and early eighteenth centuries the old, complex medieval structure of knowledge, with its formal canons of logic and carefully constructed theological schemes, was overturned by intellectuals all over Europe. In the large, general sense, the mathematically elegant Newtonian cosmos had come into vogue, based upon the works of many thinkers who were synthesized and summarized in Isaac Newton's *Principia Mathematica*, published in 1687. Newton's universe operated according to laws which could be described mathematically. Most scientists moved in the direction of eliminating theological issues from their investigations, but Newton saw nothing incompatible between his own work and studies of biblical eschatology. Moreover, intellectually alert clergy were able to incorporate the new ideas into their own thinking. Thus the Newtonian universe was usable for everyone, depending on the spirit with which it was approached.

More attractive to those seeking to reconcile the new intellectual ethos with traditional religion were the views of men like John Locke on epistemology and the freedom of the will. Particularly fascinating was the Lockean elimination of older psychological categories. Intellectual tradition had long held fast to a real separateness of the spiritual and intellectual worlds, or at least to a concept of their duality. But distinctions of mind and soul, reason and emotion, belonged to a scholastic and formalistic past that the eighteenth century was rapidly escaping. The single wholeness of mind, spirit, and emotion following from Locke's descriptions of the nature of ideation offered a new, alternative psychology.

Students of pietism and revivalism found great suggestiveness in the thought that mind and emotion could no more be out of harmony than reason and revelation could be found incompatible. If developed adequately, such a theory meant that laborious intellectual preparation for salvation—which was at the core of religious formalism—and the emotionally explosive moment of conversion were properly a single religious experience. Put crudely and simply, Locke argued that one "knew" through the emotions. To those seeking to maintain a place for traditional reason while simultaneously acknowledging the significance of the heart, the Lockean thesis offered enormous promise. Moreover, Locke maintained that human will is not a separate psychological category to which freedom or want of freedom can facilely be attributed. Volition, for Locke, became an integral property or faculty of the mind, which could not be analytically separated from others.

The new thinking and the new science could be easily accepted by the religious community of the late seventeenth and early eighteenth centuries. In 1738, on the very eve of the American Great Awakening, the comfortable bond between science and religion was concisely demonstrated in the obituaries on the death of a Dutch scientist, Herman Boerhaave. A professor of physics at Leyden, who also worked in botany, anatomy, and chemistry, Boerhaave was commemorated as a man of pious "virtue and humility" who never mentioned the "supreme being but to admire and exalt him in his work." He had studied the ancient writings of divinity and admired their "simplicity and purity of doctrine," while complaining of religion which dealt with "the subtleties of the schools."

At the University of Edinburgh resided Colin Maclaurin, whose works also synthesized religion and science in a way that offered terms for the acceptance of the new intellectual currents. "To study nature is to search into His workmanship; every new discovery opens to us a new part of His scheme." Having justified scholarly interest in the world, Maclaurin explained how that commitment could be exercised. One *must* be experimental, he said, for experimentation would reveal truth. The mental exercises of the past generations of speculative philosophers could only create uncertain systems. Experimentalism offered the present generation an avenue to truth, Maclaurin felt, and "we ought not to abuse this liberty of supposing instead of inquiring, and by imagining systems, instead of learning from observation and experience."

Here, from the technicians of science, was an avenue to the simplicity of Christianity that Boerhaave sought. With such words, the cumbersome scholastic system of the past could crumble for the religious community, as it had for the scientific. Latitudinarians and pietists alike were free to pursue the implications of new roads to knowledge. The experimental and religious impulses could be superlatively united.

As an even more strongly argued defense of the affinity of Christianity for science, Bernard Nieuwentiidt (a popular Dutch natural philosopher) published a lengthy treatise titled *The Religious Philosopher*. Nieuwentiidt confirmed God's existence by virtue of the order in the universe, and then described Him with the famous Deist metaphor of the clock maker. In keeping with the new scientific mode, the Dutchman recognized that an argument for divine reality from the observed perfection of cosmic design was an acknowledgment of empirical evidence. Yet, most arrestingly, he interpreted his scientific doctrine as an attack upon atheists who failed to exercise and to respect the obvious divine conclusions of their own sensibilities. He denounced his contemporary, Baruch Spinoza, as an atheist who had singularly depended upon logic, to the detriment of the right use of the senses.

The false conclusions of the atheists had been reached through their abuse of science, Nieuwentiidt implied, while the truth of the Bible could be proved in a simple empirical way. In fact, the Dutch scholar had taken an advanced position by placing modern empirical techniques on the side of Christian truth. At the same time, he naively relegated rationalism to hell as a false method of the atheists.

Both Nieuwentiidt and Maclaurin had attacked old means to knowledge and had offered new avenues to truth that could be used to prove the fundamentals of Christianity. That they both arrived at techniques far from revelation and essentially Deistic mattered little. The popularity of their treatises demonstrated the possible reconciliation of science and religion in the eighteenth century, from which Christians could branch out in a variety of directions. Their works appeared in the libraries of religious scholars of all interests, and were cited frequently in published sermons. For many, the attack on scholasticism probably completed the Protestant bludgeoning of Roman Catholicism that started with the Reformation. These tracts helped men move comfortably into the naturalism of the Enlightenment, while freeing them for new religious adventures.

Most critically, the religious scientists, in paving the road for increased experimentalism, had felt called upon to attack the techniques of traditional rationalism as outdated and burdensome. In one sense at least, the revisionism of modern science was close to the spirit of pietism: both denigrated formal rationalism as cold and heartless. Since the new science seemed to serve pietism as easily as it served naturalism, the vocabulary of evangelicalism harmonized comfortably with the new spirit. In Christian history, reason alone had never been an adequate means to salvation. The Protestant Reformation, as is perhaps inevitable for all revolutionary movements, tended to emphasize the nonrational, spiritual element in religion over the tedious, procedural, rational aspects. Now, two hundred years after Luther, formal reason could be further deemphasized in the name of experience and experimentalism.

Over and over in the first years of the eighteenth century, clergymen reiterated the need for religious experience. They sought a profound sense of harmony with God which rested upon faith and not reason. In a century of experimental science and "experiential" knowledge, the realms of religion and science did not mean quite the same thing by the term "experimental." But a single vocabulary helped to bring science and religion together. Just as the scientist accepted nothing simply because it was written in a book, so the individual could not rely upon "Christian knowledge." The scientist insisted upon discovering the operations of natural laws through the personal experience of experiment, while many Christians came to seek God through the personal experiment of experience. The compatibility was important.

CHAPTER THREE

Pietism in America

*Alas Hearers! That yet walk in the ways of Sin, and
will not leave them, but do love them, and live in
them with Pleasure; You likewise who walk in the
Ways of Self Righteousness, trusting upon your
Heart, upon your good intentions, and the like, you
also who are come no farther than upon the way of
Civility and external Godliness, but know nothing of
any true Change, are not as yet regenerated and
renewed, O here is sorrow full News! for the end of
your way is Death: although your Way seemeth right
unto you, yet the End thereof are the Ways of Death,
O think upon it well what Wretchedness that herein is
included for you, if it might be a means for your
Conviction and Conversion.*

—Theodorus J. Frelinghuysen, "A MIRROUR that
Flatereth not, BEING A Serious Discourse to
discover false Grounds, and an Admonition, to
procede with Zeal in the narrow Way of Godliness"

America was never isolated from the currents of intellectual change. It followed the shifting mood of Protestantism and made contact with the pietist leaders of the Continent. European pietism struck a respondent chord in the Calvinistic traditions of several major American denominations, Puritan, Presbyterian, and Reformed. Calvinistic religion, with its dedication to a personal search for salvation, always tottered on the verge of pietistic enthusiasm. The tendency was perhaps most pronounced in the New England religious tradition, but the Puritans were not America's only heirs of the theology of John Calvin. An emphasis on the inscrutability of God, the unconditional election of the saints, and original sin characterized Presbyterianism as well as the German and Dutch Reformed churches of the Middle Colonies. Not surprisingly, these were the denominations in America which led in pressing pietistic principles. By the early 1730s, pietism had won a foothold and had begun to establish the positive intellectual basis conducive to revivalism.

Pietism and the Mather Faction in New England

The committed Puritan spent endless hours in self-examination as part of his preparation for salvation. He read Scripture and contemplated each passage carefully, for the Bible could bring him closer to Christ. A soul-searching private confession of ever-present sin also preoccupied him. Humiliation at the sinful nature of man and horror in the face of eternal damnation were supposed to accompany self-scrutiny, as the Puritan sought some evidence of grace in his soul. Was he truly one of the elect? No one could ever be certain. A conversion experience which could be related to peers might lead to membership in the temporal church, but might be false, self-delusive, and hypocritical. The highly personal and sensitive self-examination demanded by Puritan tradition was never far removed from the unchecked and emotional experience that would be at the center of the Great Awakening.

Most divines left some self-conscious record of the personal contemplation expected of them. Many, like Ebenezer Parkman of Westborough, mechanically logged their contemplative sessions in a diary:

> Besides enlarging my Devotions according to my Custom on this Day, (in Praises for the Divine Mercies through my Life and particularly through this Year past, in reviewing my Life and humbling my Self for my past iniquitys, Vanitys, impuritys and impietys, and reading such suitable passages of Sacred Scripture as Ps. 145, Dan 9, Ps. 103 and Job 14, p.m.), I made it considerably my Business to try and prove my Self whether I have indeed had a work of Grace Savingly wrought in my heart.

Others, like Cotton Mather, were more passionate:

> Being prostrate in the Dust on my Study-floor, after many Fears of a sad, heavy, woful Heart, that the Holy Spirit of the Lord Jesus Christ, grieved by my Miscarriages, would forsake mee utterly, that Spirit of the Lord made an inexpressible Descent upon mee. A stream of tears gushed out of my Eyes, upon my Floor, while I had my Soul inexpressibly irradiated with Assurances, of especially two or three Things, bore in upon mee.

But some such efforts were expected of all would-be saints.

For all Calvinists, whether Puritan, Presbyterian, or Reformed, passage through life traditionally focused on a search for salvation. The mark of the successful quest, however tenuous, came with a conversion experience. In the search for that experience, God was a vital force perched just out of sight. Daily life was a constant challenge, full of trials and punishments. Death was the final test. Ever-present providence—for both the individual and society —dominated all explanation of experience. Only an insistence upon formal reason and the demand for cogent evidence of conversion kept the inherent passion in check. European pietism could help remove the restrictions, by indicating that reason and emotion were not incompatible.

Not surprisingly, the first recorded contact of American religion with European pietism came through Cotton Mather, the great arbiter of Puritanism. Always sensitive to changed moods, and profoundly frustrated by a seeming decline of Puritanism, Mather helped to bring New England into the eighteenth century with large doses of the most modern Old World thinking. In 1709 he opened a correspondence with Augustus Francke (somewhat presumptuously described to others as "my good friend Francke"). Mather's conviction of the imminence of the millennium contributed to the eagerness with which he joined Francke in the search for a pious community. Apparently discovering Francke's words almost as soon as they were translated into English, the New Englander predicted a worldwide revival stimulated by the Germans:

> The world begins to feel a warmth from the fire of God, which thus flames in the heart of Germany, beginning to extend into many regions. The whole world will e're long be sensible of it!

And Cotton Mather hoped to be a part of the new conflagration.

Speaking as the self-proclaimed leader of the New World intellectuals, Mather never thought of himself as a provincial American. His sensitivity to the work being done in Germany and to the words coming from the German religious leaders was in part a British dissenter's response. As England republished its early calls for religious concern and discovered the Continental pietists and Francke, Mather heard of them as well. His correspondence with those in the mother country who were absorbing the new spirit was vital. But Mather's particular application of pietism focused naturally on New England. He wrote pietist tracts himself and confided to his diary that such essays would mark a "new American pietism."

In the spirit of the pietists and in the tradition of the English societies, Mather hoped to rally the New England community around the popular public problem of social behavior. The focus would be on the personalized religious emphasis of the German example. Each man's search for salvation had social implications for his behavior. And preparation for salvation could be observed, in part, in obvious social concerns.

Mather attempted to organize a society along sound pietistic lines in *Bonifacius, An Essay Upon the Good That is to be Devised and Designed for Those Who Desire . . . To Do Good While They Live*. In his preface, Mather concentrated on the major issue. The world could be a better place, he argued, and an intelligent man must feel a profound sense of responsibility to improve it. The individual's duty was "to heal the disorders, and help the distresses of the miserable world." Such a view was hardly original, but for New England it acknowledged a shift in thought. The world would no longer be quietly accepted as a place or time of trial in preparation for the hereafter. Secular disorders and distresses could and should be attacked by pious men. "Mankind," Mather wrote, "may be better for our actions." He brought together the optimism of a new century and the piety of a new religious attitude. What that union might bring could not be predicted with accuracy when Mather published *Bonifacius* in 1710. Certainly a renewed interest in religion was part of his purpose, and in his own mind he woud link his work with that of the German pietists.

With great care Mather placed the concern for good conduct into a proper New England theological framework. The first step for anyone who sought to do good would be a rebirth. Justification must come first, for without it there could be no good works. From such a foundation, Mather could launch into the specifics of humanitarianism. Like William Law, he balanced social work with the personal spiritual search. He also offered specific advice, dividing his essay by professions: minister, schoolmaster, physician. He urged Christianizing the slaves and assisting the suffering poor. Visit them, he said, comfort them, advise them, and provide alms for them.

Visit, comfort, advise, and provide alms. Such was "social concern" for American pietism. Like most Old World leaders of the movement, Cotton Mather had a very limited concept of the possibility of reform. In large measure his view followed naturally from his emphasis on the importance of eternal salvation and his commitment to divine election. Mortal life was only a temporary state, and God had ordained man's place in it. The good Christian was enjoined by the Bible to ameliorate the state of the unfortunate, but not to alter it.

Pietism caught little of the spirit of radical Protestantism arising from the Reformation or the civil wars in Europe and England. In modern terms, Cotton Mather (like pietism generally), was "liberal" rather than "radical." He sought to scold the social order, not to overthrow it. He emphasized individual regeneration rather than social reconstruction. When pietism and evangelicalism joined hands in the Great Awakening, the resultant reform impulse was of the same order. A radical reconstruction of society, or elimination of slavery or poverty by social action, were never really part of mainstream pietism. The emphasis was on the elimination of personal rather than social sin. Drunkenness, rather than oppression, was the typical target. Pietism's radical posture was for another world, not this one.

Cotton Mather tried to live by his own injunction to do good. After 1710 he often marked his diary entries "GD," and then carefully catalogued the good he had done: encouraged children to read from a book of piety, gave a book of religious instruction to a neglected nephew, decided to revive a disbanded "society for the suppression of disorder," tried to heal the discord of the Salem church, helped the poor victims of a fire. He continued to mark selected diary entries "GD" until his death. Many criticized his efforts as interferences, but Mather never ceased.

The entire Mather faction, which was substantial in the Boston area, quickly came to its leader's support. The urging to better behavior, instigated by Mather, merged imperceptibly into the Great Awakening. His followers slowly but easily embraced a "vital piety" which gradually moved them away from the traditional Puritan emphasis on formal reason and logic. The orthodox demands for rational forms in the pursuit of personal salvation could never be abandoned, but a growing concern for a spiritual state resting upon the emotions began to mark the sermons of the period. The Puritan continued his usual insistence upon learning, reading, and thinking, but a first concern became his "own heart."

The earliest evidence of a shift into pietism appeared as an appeal for a renewed religious interest. No one made the call more clearly than the "weeping parson," Joseph Sewall, of the Old South Church in Boston. Sewall, son of the famous diarist, issued warnings to his congregation to prepare for the day of judgment. His call was part of that renewed interest in millenarianism fostered by Cotton Mather. Then, in response to a warning from God in the earthquake of 1727, Sewall called out again for "the work of reformation." The change was a subtle one of emphasis. None could point to a concrete alteration in doctrine, nor any move that could be labeled as innovation. As in England, greater personal and emotional concern in religious life, and more active social involvement, seemed characteristic of the age.

John Webb, pastor of Boston's New North Church, complemented Joseph Sewall's call for reformation. "The faith of a Christian is not like the faith of a philosopher," he warned. It could not be "confined to the head but it extends to the heart." Thomas Prince, Sewall's co-pastor at the Old South Church and leader of the Mather faction after the patriarch's death, caught the new mood even earlier than Webb. He may, in fact, have assisted in bringing others to it. As early as 1718, Prince was insisting that "in conversion there is a great alteration in us." The first concern for those seeking salvation, he argued, is to seek that alteration through a change of one's "own heart." In 1721 the entire Mather faction united in the face of a smallpox crisis to offer *A Course of Sermons on Early Piety*. Following an introduction by the venerable Increase Mather, Cotton explained that one who was "brought home to God" would have "his affections brought into order."

The Mather shift was subtle and complex. It insisted on uniting piety and social concern; it sought changes of heart without comprehending how to produce them in others. But elsewhere in America a more single-minded pietism was emerging.

Middle Colony Pietism: The Dutch Reformed Church

Over roughly the same time span that saw Cotton Mather and those Puritan clergy who followed his lead move gradually toward a posture of pietism, the Middle Colonies developed their own pietism, beginning in the Dutch Reformed church. The relationship with European pietism was not, as in the case of Mather, a second-hand one based upon reading and correspondence. In New York and New Jersey the introduction of Continental pietism was direct, embodied in Bernardus Freeman and Theodorus Frelinghuysen.

Freeman had come to the New World under peculiar circumstances, suggesting an early attachment to religious innovation. He had arrived in New York in 1705 in response to a clandestine call from one faction of a badly divided Dutch colony at Albany.

Evert Bancker, a leading layman of the church, had contacted his brother William, an Amsterdam merchant, to request a clergyman whose sympathies were catholic enough to encompass pietism. Although the Classis of Amsterdam held responsibility for the supply and appointment of clergy to the New World (the Dutch had no seminaries or church government in America), the merchant bypassed it. Freeman was not acceptable to the traditionalist Amsterdam Classis; so Bancker hurried him off to the university town of Lingen in Westphalia for ordination. Westphalia was an area of considerable pietist strength, which may explain both the strategy of Bancker and the leanings of Freeman. Meanwhile another faction at Albany called a minister in the approved fashion from the Classis of Amsterdam. Both men sailed for the New World.

Once both ministers were in New York in direct competition, Freeman was rejected at Albany. He settled instead at Schenectady. Clergy were too scarce in the colonies among those denominations relying on European supply for Freeman to be utterly rejected, whatever his peculiarities. From the beginning, Dominie Freeman proved to be an independent soul, fostering controversy. Eventually he moved to Long Island, again with unusual machinations surrounding the action. Above all, he refused to acknowledge the discipline of the Classis of Amsterdam, and turned to the British colonial government for his authority to preach. The Amsterdam Classis could only comment that "his conduct appears very strange to us."

With apparent calculation, some Dutch-speaking settlers along the Raritan River in New Jersey turned to Freeman when they sought a clergyman to serve their scattered settlements. And Freeman turned to his old friend Bancker and another Amsterdam merchant. Perhaps with memory of the troubles surrounding Freeman's appointment, the Amsterdam agents carefully prepared to serve their American clients. When the two merchants appeared before the Amsterdam Classis to present the request from Raritan, they had a man waiting in the wings: Theodorus Jacob Frelinghuysen, a German who had formerly served as minister in East Friesland and then as co-pastor at Euckbuyzen. He appeared the moment the Classis learned of the merchants' charge. Properly equipped with testimonials from an impressive array of clergymen attesting to his orthodoxy, Frelinghuysen promised appropriate loyalty to the church and Classis and was quickly approved. Once at sea, however, the good reverend abandoned some of his calculated reserve before the Classis, and in conversation he condemned most of the clergy of Holland as unconverted, particularly those of Amsterdam.

Frelinghuysen landed in New York City in January 1720. After a brief display of his pulpit talents, which gave his fellow clergy some notion of the new preacher in their midst, he pushed on to New Jersey to serve as the traveling parson for three churches. Unlike Cotton Mather's emphasis on both pietism and social concern for others, Frelinghuysen focused chiefly on the individual's "heart." Almost immediately upon arrival in the Raritan Valley, he began to complain of the state of religion in the area and called upon his hearers for a "new heart." European pietism had arrived in New Jersey.

Demanding greater attention to one's religious state than had been asked in the past, Frelinghuysen warned that those who had not been saved but who acted complacently in their church lives were in the greatest danger of damnation. Most startling, he denied communion to many—even members of his church consistory—as unregenerate. Before long, Frelinghuysen had split his church and initiated one of the longest and most bitter ecclesiastical disputes in colonial history.

Controversy lingered on when Frelinghuysen died in 1747 and the Great Awakening's excitement had largely faded. The dissidents who left the church did not return until 1751. Although the Raritan controversy has often been associated with the early beginnings of the Great Awakening, the issue was not revivalism but pietism European style. In Raritan, Frelinghuysen was not engaged in sweeping great numbers into the church but in keeping people out.

The Raritan dominie had come from the Old World to show his countrymen in the New World how depraved they were, and to teach them the exquisite beauty of rebirth. His attack on the traditional formalism of the Reformed church shattered its tranquillity for two generations. But his pietistic preaching satisfied many in his congregation, as well as some Englishmen who found new meaning in the frontier austerity of their lives and new purpose in what seemed an uncertain providence. The religious message of Frelinghuysen was utterly personal, demanding only a thorough examination of the individual's position vis-à-vis God. But he caused only regional excitement and produced few converts. New England heard vague rumors of his presence, but Frelinghuysen was more pietist than revivalist, and was limited by the language barrier.

One important English-speaking family *did* come into direct and significant contact with the Raritan dominie. This was the Tennent family, who introduced pietism to American Presbyterianism.

Middle Colony Pietism: The Presbyterian Church

The family of William Tennent arrived in America in 1718 as part of the Scots-Irish wave of migration of the time. William had graduated from the University of Edinburgh and been ordained a priest of the Church of Ireland. Once in America, and perhaps under the influence of a Presbyterian wife, he abandoned his former church to ask the Presbyterian Synod for admission as a minister. His explanation for leaving the Irish Anglican communion indicated a Calvinistic inclination and hinted at the future direction of his thought. Tennent explained that he could accept neither the hierarchy nor the "ceremonial way of worship." Perhaps more significantly, he complained of lax doctrine in the Church of Ireland, which he labeled "inconsistent with the eternal purpose of God, and an encouragement of vice." It is not clear whether he understood that the American Presbyterians were themselves fairly latitudinarian. In any event, opposition to Anglicanism could only please the Presbyterians, and neither party examined each other's views very carefully. Suffering a serious shortage of clergy as more and more parishioners of their persuasion migrated from the Old World, the Presbyterian Synod appealed constantly to its brethren in the British Isles for men and money. Thus William Tennent was accepted into the American ministry.

Frustrated in an attempt to achieve the presidency of Yale, William tried to supply sorely needed Presbyterian clergy by training his sons and others at home. This venture gradually expanded into the famous "Log College," which after 1727 was located in Tennent's parish of Neshaminy, Bucks County, Pennsylvania. Gilbert, the eldest Tennent son, moved from the Log College to Yale. He then accepted a call from New Brunswick, New Jersey, and became a neighbor of Jacob Frelinghuysen.

Gilbert Tennent was profoundly impressed by Frelinghuysen's pulpit techniques and pietism. The two men soon became close friends, and linguistic, ethnic, and denominational differences quickly faded as they united against the unrepented sins of their parishioners. On a number of occasions Tennent and Frelinghuysen appeared together in the pulpit, the former preaching in English and the latter in Dutch. By 1730, pietism had become a recognizable force in the Presbyterian church.

New England Pietism: Ferris and Edwards

Although the Boston of Cotton Mather sometimes seemed the center of New England, pietism began to flourish outside the Massachusetts capital. Yale College was affected around 1730, apparently a result of local forces as much as external intellectual influences. A small group in the little town of New Medford, Connecticut, had in 1726 enjoyed a spiritual revival. It broke away from the local church, claiming an immediate indwelling of the spirit of God that resulted in direct communication from Him. Contemporaries quickly labeled the schismatics "Quakers." One young rebel, David Ferris, stood out from the rest, for he sought a formal education at Yale, and he arrived in New Haven for the 1729 college term.

Ferris remained quiet at first, but soon fell in with a group of students who had been reading pietistic authors. A club was formed to express their religious concerns. Ferris quickly became a leader, adding to the intellectual understanding of pietism some actual emotional experience. He insisted upon the immediate operation of the Holy Spirit to produce sudden conversions and assurance of a sanctified state. As was true elsewhere in the Protestant world, young men at the colonial college of Yale were concerned for religious knowledge through nonformalistic means.

The club which Ferris led was an indigenous American counterpart of the more famous Oxford group which included the Wesleys and George Whitefield.

As Yale bubbled with new religious notions, one of its graduates appeared in 1731 as a voice for pietistic reform. In that year, Jonathan Edwards traveled from his pulpit in the Connecticut Valley to Boston, the Puritan capital, where he delivered a Thursday lecture from the pulpit of the First Church. Edwards was part of the Puritan clerical aristocracy, non-Boston branch. His grandfather, Solomon Stoddard, had been the spiritual (and some said secular) dictator of western Massachusetts and adjoining Connecticut, and a worthy lifelong opponent of Cotton Mather. As grandson of Mather's old enemy and a graduate of Yale, Edwards attracted a large and curious Boston audience.

In his lecture sermon Edwards spoke simply and undramatically. He reminded New England of man's absolute dependence upon God for salvation, thus recalling the Puritans' Calvinist past. At the same time, he set aside the continual Puritan problem of a personal quest for salvation. Instead, he cried out in traditional language for more awareness of man's utter dependence upon Christ. Rely not on yourself, but on Him. At the moment, the audience was fascinated by what seemed to be harsh Calvinism reincarnate. Few saw the new and mystical avenue to joy that underlay Edwards' orthodox language.

Boston clergymen Thomas Prince and William Cooper expressed their delight with the Edwards sermon in a preface to its printed edition: "If the Doctrine of Grace is ever lost then so is piety. We are thus happy to see such a young man arise from Among us, to supply God's churches." Prince and his proto-pietist faction had for years been crying out against the decline in religious interest, and this included a loss of emphasis upon an omnipotent God. Prince had warned that in a world full of snares there is no true beauty, only an arena of trial. Sadly, he told of the lost soul who would finally repent in terror on his death bed. For those who repented so late no hope could be held. Joseph Sewall added that men must fear worldly temptation and listen to God's threats.

In Edwards a new and influential ally had appeared from an unexpected quarter, and the preface to the Thursday sermon made the reason for the alliance explicit: "For in proportion to the sense we have of our dependence on the sovereign God for all of the good we want, will be our application to him, our trust in him, our fear to offend him." That there could be joy in the spiritual release to be gained from Edwards' unfettered dependence upon Christ went unrecognized.

The German Pietists in America

As men like Gilbert Tennent and Jonathan Edwards gained stature in the 1730s, the activities of German pietists and their preachers accelerated both in Pennsylvania and the Deep South, particularly in Georgia. German pietists had been immigrating to America since the 1680s. The first Germans in Pennsylvania included a band of Mennonites and German Quakers, who founded Germantown in 1683. Ten years later, forty highly educated pietists arrived in Pennsylvania. Called the Order of the Woman in the Wilderness, they waited in the forest for the millennium. In 1719, twenty families of Dunkers migrated, and soon were joined by Schwenckfelders and Moravians.

The German migrants, including the pietists, experienced the usual difficulties of European settlers in the New World. Wilderness conditions were strange and difficult, and material concerns took priority over religious matters. Moreover, the migrants found themselves under strong pressures to assimilate to a predominantly British society. A shortage of clergymen seemed a large part of the general difficulty, and as the Germans prospered they called to the Old World for preachers. In 1736, for example, A. G. Spangenberg of the Moravian Brethren was sent to Pennsylvania in response to a request from colonists "for a couple of Brethren to minister to their own physical and spiritual well-being and in addition to see that a way might be prepared for the Lord should He grant this land to experience a gracious visitation." Spangenberg's visit was sufficiently successful to induce him to write back to the leader of the Moravians in Europe, Count Ludwig Zinzendorf, urging a visit to Pennsylvania. Zinzendorf responded to the pleas and arrived in America in November 1741, amid the excitement of the Great Awakening.

Before 1740, however, the German pietists' activities were limited largely to their own countrymen and various sympathetic English-speaking sectarians. Spangenberg "received many a visit from people of varied persuasions: Baptists, Quakers, the Sabbatarians of Ephrata, and Separatists." Both a defensive cultural attitude and the language barrier tended to isolate the German pietists from their English-speaking colleagues. Certainly adherents of the major Calvinistic denominations in America remained outside the appeal of the German pietist sects at this time.

All in all, it was clear by the 1730s that concern for a more experimental religious expression was growing throughout the American colonies. Pietism was preparing the way for revivalism.

CHAPTER FOUR

Preparations for the Awakening

*God has also seemed to have gone out of his usual
way, in the quickness of his work, and the swift
progress his spirit has made in his operations on the
hearts of many. It is wonderful that persons should
be so suddenly, and yet so greatly changed. Many
have been taken from a loose and careless way of
living, and seized with strong convictions of their
guilt and misery, and in a very little time old things
have passed away, and all things have become new
with them.*

*—Jonathan Edwards, A Faithful Narrative of the
Surprising Work of God, 1737*

Preachers like Jonathan Edwards and Jacob Frelinghuysen, through their reemphasis upon Calvin's omnipotent God, threatened much of the early-eighteenth-century perception of the means of conversion. For Edwards, the focus was God's immediate and somewhat mysterious influence rather than Christian knowledge and concern. A subtle shift in sermon style to accompany this new emphasis had been occurring, and would continue, but pietism was not automatically evangelistic, and revival was not its inevitable result. However, the problems which faced those clergymen, who were turning to pietism, made the possibility of revivalism much more likely.

The growing strength of pietism embodied an international movement of spiritual reform. It was intended to counter the problems of the world as perceived by clergymen in many nations. Probably no clerics were more conscious of the need for reform than those of America, and particularly in the Calvinistic denominations of the Northern colonies. These clergymen preached sermons by the dozen exhorting their people to cease their conflict with each other, to live more simply, to return to the greater faith and more stable ways of the past. These "jeremiads," as they have been called, fell on deaf ears in the 1730s. No one listened, because the clergy had been saying the same things for over half a century. The sense of urgency had long since disappeared from the message.

Religious leadership and authority seemed to be eroding throughout the colonies. The Puritan clergy of New England had lost their dominance, the Calvinist clergy of the Middle Colonies had not achieved dominance, and the Anglican clergy of the South had stoically accepted the belief that they could never aspire to leadership. Even among the Quakers, who did not have a formal ministry, lay preachers despaired at the loss of religious concern, partly to the secular world and partly to an inward-looking tribalism which became characteristic of American Quakerism. The credibility of religion as a vital force in colonial America seemed at a low ebb in the 1730s. The ministry felt it acutely, and the people sensed it. As the spokesmen for religion, many clergymen were not prepared either to give up on the churches or to surrender their own status, which was so dependent upon the churches.

The problems were many and severe, and can be grouped roughly into two categories. There were those matters which could only with difficulty be articulated publicly, and in many cases they were perhaps not clearly recognized privately. Then came those ills which were usually alluded to under the catch-phrase "Arminianism."

The Loss of Clerical Leadership

Cotton Mather had long been one of the leaders in the New England battle against the erosion of clerical influence. Massachusetts seemed the center of the struggle, since religion and its ministers had been more important in the Bay Colony than anywhere else in America. But the alien forces were more general. Secular political forces gained influence following the Glorious Revolution. A relaxed and enlightened spirit of religious latitudinarianism was abroad. Material prosperity seemed to draw many away from a single-minded concern with religious matters. The colleges were corrupted. These were all enemies which could be openly attacked, and were from scores of pulpits. Their local manifestations were less easy to handle.

Perhaps the most critical point among the unarticulated problems was the increasing localized domination by laymen over ministerial appointment and financial support. In no American colony did the state contribute money directly to religion. Instead, even in colonies with "established churches," the state merely authorized the collection of local taxes for ecclesiastical purposes. There were no large endowments to support religion; few Americans could afford to become patrons of churches, as did European princes and noblemen. As a result, clergymen of all American denominations received their salaries and the funds for maintenance of the church from local congregations, either through taxes or private contributions. And taxpayers and contributors both felt, as one Massachusetts man put it early in the eighteenth century, that they wanted "all the Benefit of their money."

One of the benefits which laymen expected was a say in the

government of the church. The ministers, who were ordained of God, and specially called and educated, would naturally have preferred to lead their congregations. New England Puritanism failed to maintain what one cleric had called "a silent democracy in the face of a speaking aristocracy." The Lutheran leader, Henry Muhlenberg, complained: "It is easier to be a cowherd or a shepherd in many places in Germany than to be a preacher here, where every peasant wants to act the part of a patron of the parish, for which he has neither the intelligence nor the skill." Jacob Frelinghuysen's academic degrees and scholarly attainments did not prevent ordinary members of his Raritan congregation from opposing him when he threatened their interests.

In Virginia the local vestry, dominated by the leading families in the parish, had rendered impotent virtually every Anglican clergyman in the colony. While New England and even Dutch Reformed ministers might struggle with their parishioners, the clergy in Virginia silently acquiesced. The Virginia assembly cavalierly tinkered with the value of the tobacco in which ministers received their salaries and not until well after the Great Awakening did the clergy protest. And then, in the famous "Parson's Cause" case, Patrick Henry's father found that a strong legal case was cast aside by a jury of his peers.

Some ministers were able to maintain their authority in the face of threats posed by the laity, but most were not. In many denominations, the absence of colonial educational facilities and the necessity of traveling to Europe to gain formal ordination to the ministry led to the wholesale importation of European clergymen. Many left Europe because they had no future there. Even when immigrant ministers had outstanding capacities and abilities—as did William Tennent and Jacob Frelinghuysen—they faced a long period of adjustment to American conditions. Only New England's two colleges trained a native clergy. And by the eighteenth century, the demands of an expanding population and the opportunities for advancement elsewhere in a prosperous society had led to debasement of the general ranks of the Puritan clergy. Too many men with only ordinary intellectual and moral attainments had been ordained to New England churches. Such men were in no position to assert clerical leadership.

Most clergymen of ordinary talent failed to meet the challenge of secularism inherent in an increasingly vocal laity that controlled the power of the purse. They not only ceased struggling for ecclesiastical power, but they played it safe spiritually as well. Unless one were a Jonathan Edwards, it was easier to take refuge behind doctrines and practices which made few demands on parishioners than to insist on standards which few could meet. Ministers settled for stylized sermons of biblical exegesis or ethical exhortation. They permitted, without challenge, the growth of ecclesiastical practices which appealed to the widest possible audience.

In New England, for example, by 1740 virtually every inhabitant could gain baptism, despite the traditional Puritan objection to an Anglican/Catholic emphasis upon a comprehensive church. Puritanism in America had begun by insisting that only the children of the saints were entitled to the sacrament. Then the so-called "halfway covenant" had extended baptism to descendants of saints. Liberal interpretation of the halfway practice allowed most New Englanders to be baptized, but few Puritan ministers would refuse the sacrament even to those who could claim no saintly ancestry. How could a minister deny baptism to the children of one of his ratepayers? How could a minister remain independent when those who paid the bills became vocal?

The Growth of "Arminianism"

Clergymen could be found everywhere in America to agree with the sentiments of a piece in the *South Carolina Gazette* for 1732: "There is a Sort of Thrift or Good-Husbandry in moral Life, which does not throw away any single Action, but makes every one go as far as it can. It multiplies the Means of Salvation, encreases the Number of our Virtues, and diminishes that of our Vices." Moral good-husbandry—the very phrase calls to mind the attitude of men like Benjamin Franklin—emphasized good works as a means of salvation. In 1722 James Blair, the Anglican Commissary of Virginia, published 117 sermons on the Sermon on the Mount. Like the pietists, he too sought a "new man." But for Blair the new man was the moral man. He could not understand those who emphasized conversion, "as if they knew of some other Way of being saved by inward Acts of Faith and Repentance, without the conscientious Practice of Moral Duties." Blair allowed that morality includes "the inward Principle too of the Love and Fear of God; and a careful watching of our Hearts and Thoughts, and keeping a good Conscience before God." While Blair and the pietists could agree that the new man should be gracious and moral, Blair chose to emphasize the morality and the pietists the graciousness.

Anglicans in the North—many of whom were converts from other denominations—tended to stress self-consciously the traditions of the mother church of England more than did the Virginia ministry. But all Anglicans could agree on moral good-husbandry. So too, claimed the pietist critics, could many clergy in all denominations. A permissive spirit and moral emphasis were part of what contemporaries meant when they used the term "Arminianism." Arminius was a seventeenth-century theologian of great intellect, and when properly used in reference to his teachings, "Arminianism" had a technical and limited meaning. In general usage, however, "Arminianism" referred derogatorily to any undue emphasis upon works and morality at the expense of saving faith.

Moral good-husbandry was part of what John White had in mind when he castigated Arminianism in a 1734 pamphlet titled *New England Lamentations*. White was related by marriage to great Puritans such as John Wise and the Mathers. His jeremiad called for all New Englanders to return to the church with the dedication of their fathers:

> While they are cold and careless as to the Concerns of their Souls, and Eternity; they are over-heated, and deeply engaged in their Affections towards the Profits, Pleasures, and Preferments of the World. . . . When a professing People cast off Fear, tis a sad Occasion of the decay of Godliness.

White's *Lamentations* won the endorsement of most Boston ministers with pietist leanings. Peter Thacher (minister of the New North Church in Boston), Joseph Sewall, Thomas Prince, John Webb, William Cooper, and Thomas Foxcroft all signed a recommendation for White's tract.

Though his readers undoubtedly recognized White's "Arminianism" as a general term of opprobrium, they also understood its special connection with the Church of England. While many Puritan clergymen may quietly have practiced moral good-husbandry, only a few had been willing to admit it openly. These offenders were quickly isolated. But leaders of the newly resurgent Anglican denomination in New England and the Middle Colonies were under no constraints. They could flaunt their moralism openly, particularly after 1722, when the rector of Yale College, Timothy Cutler, and several of his tutors, including Samuel Johnson, publicly declared their attachment to Anglicanism. The result, according to one hostile observer, was the infection of a whole generation of college graduates with "Arminian and Prelatical Notions."

Like many converts, the Yale men quickly became aggressive and extreme. They attempted to infiltrate the Harvard board of overseers; they denied the validity of all Congregational and Presbyterian ordinations; they defended the liturgy of the church and attacked its absence among dissenters. Unlike Anglicanism in the South, the Church of England in the Northern colonies was loud and vociferous, and was led by men who would brook no compromises with the traditional teachings of the church. Although they might deny being Arminians (Arminius, after all, was a Dutch Calvinist), they certainly opposed predestination and emphasized morality. They were also root-and-branch enemies of enthusiasm and pietism in any form. Like their clergymen, most Anglican laymen in the North had begun in some other denomination.

Thus conversion to Anglicanism included a conscious rejection of most aspects of religious experience which would be associated with the Great Awakening. Colonial Anglicanism, especially north of Virginia, would always remain outside revivalism. Significantly, however, Anglican apostasy was the extreme example of what could happen—and was happening—to churches which had fallen away from basic principles. By the 1730s the Church of England was gaining converts everywhere. With decline came division.

The clergy of the North increasingly felt the necessity of the need for regeneration. Some agency—who else but God?—must bring to the people a spiritual awakening which would arrest decline and division. If only God would make the people care! If their hearts could be truly affected, perhaps the people would pay attention to their pastors. Clerical authority would be restored. The drift to Anglicanism and beyond would be arrested. The trick was to turn pietism evangelical. This happened relatively spontaneously, so to speak, over a long period of time.

The Rise of Revivalism and Evangelicalism

Outbreaks of spiritual concern and sudden upsurges in church attendance, and even membership, were common in the American colonies before 1740. But contemporaries did not view sporadic revivals as part of a general movement. They were either connected with the successful activities of individual pastors or with external events—usually natural catastrophes—which wreaked temporary fear in the hearts of the public. The elements of revivalism were always present in American life. Only gradually did general publicity, clerical cooperation, and conscious evangelicalism coalesce. By the 1730s such factors were being combined.

In the deeply introspective community of New England the clergy subjected every issue to careful literary examination, according to the rules of their tradition. A society in covenant with God responded daily to the dispensations of divine providence. An omnipresent God punished His people for their failings with epidemics and earthquakes, and He rewarded their displays of piety with prosperity and victory in battle. God could be appealed to through the testimony of a lesson learned. He had to be shown proper appreciation of His blessings. Accordingly, days of humiliation and thanksgiving punctuated New England life. Rises and declines in religious excitement were measured against daily events. In such an environment, proper form demanded complaints against religious decline and calls for revival. Periodically a minor awakening in religious interest would occur.

One such revival occurred in Taunton, Massachusetts, under the ministry of Samuel Danforth. A patriarch of his church, Danforth had published "An Astronomical Description" of a comet in

1664, learnedly discussing its parallax in order to offer a "Brief *Theological Application* of this strange and notable *Appearance* in the *Heavens.*" For Danforth, comets were "Portentous *and* [a] Signal of *great and notable Changes.*" In 1704 and 1705, Danforth combined his community's reaffirmation of its obligations to God with "Some awful Deaths and Amazing Providences" to produce a number of conversions "attended with more than the usual degrees of horror." He formed small, regular "Meetings for Prayer" and insisted on promises to reform "Idleness, unnecessary frequenting [of] Houses of Public entertainment, irreverant behaviour in public Worship, Neglect of family prayer, Promise breaking and walking with slanderers, and Reproachers of others." Danforth embodied the fusion of pietism, interest in science, and concern for public morality exemplified by Josiah Woodward in England at about the same time. But his revival remained local.

Another church patriarch, in western Massachusetts, produced similar results under different circumstances. Solomon Stoddard, minister of Northampton and grandfather of Jonathan Edwards, was leader of a movement within New England Puritanism to break with the traditions Danforth was exploiting. Instead of insisting on "horrible" conversions, Stoddard preferred to permit anyone who understood the doctrines of the church and was not openly "vicious" in behavior to become a member. The results of his calls for the people to join the church were five wellspaced "harvests" of souls between 1680 and 1719. According to his grandson, the harvests were particularly heavy among the young. What Stoddard did was regularly bring a new generation into his church.

Beyond local revivals such as those in Taunton and Northampton, all natural calamities had the effect of filling the churches for the moment. When such events excited public concern, calls for repentance and commitment to God gained considerable momentum. The earthquake of 1727 was particularly distressing, and all over America the clergy exploited the event as a signal from God of the need for reform. For a brief period, pastors preached to crowded and attentive congregations. They reaped the results of their emphasis on the event of the moment in suddenly increased admissions to church membership and baptisms. But the clergy understood the limitations of such exploitation; they knew that church attendance would soon be back to normal when such fears were forgotten.

Early New England revivalism, whether a purely local phenomenon as in Taunton or general as with the 1727 earthquake, was not normally beset with controversy and factional dissension. Conflict was absent largely because revival did not involve external factors but was simply a development of locally accepted values and traditions. In the Middle Colonies, however, the alliance of Frelinghuysen and Gilbert Tennent was more aggressive. The two not only fought unrepented sin in their own parishes but were willing to take the battle abroad. They probably traveled together to the little village of Freehold, New Jersey, a community where Scots-Irish immigrants had found religious freedom in the seventeenth century and had been joined by some Dutch who were escaping the omnipresent English in New York. The tiny town sat on the fringes of colonial settlement; only the Toms River lay between it and the uninhabited Pine Barrens. Surrounded by forests and meadows, the Dutch Reformed and the English-speaking Presbyterians each had a church. Since 1707 they had shared a single clergyman, Joseph Morgan. Here in Freehold was played out a drama which would be repeated many times in America after 1740.

Joseph Morgan was a third-generation American who had begun his ministry in Greenwich, Connecticut. He then moved to Westchester County, New York. The royal governor found him undesirably nonconformist and shipped him home to Greenwich. But his congregation soon tired of Morgan and accused him of neglecting parish duties for the sake of his investment in a grist mill. Eventually he migrated to New Jersey, to assume his dual role in Freehold. Nothing is known of Morgan's educational background, for his name appears on none of the colonial college lists, but he seems to have had some intellectual pretensions, for he published more than most ministers. Morgan dabbled in theoretical science and even offered technological suggestions to the Royal Navy. Undoubtedly argumentative and independent, Morgan held his Freehold posts for twenty years. Even his enemies admitted he was a man of "acknowledged orthodoxy and exemplary character." But he was not very inspiring.

Morgan's parish was a typical agrarian community, with little economic differentiation and few intellectual pretensions. His parishioners worked diligently to gather small farm-estates. They knew the reality of the harsh Calvinistic world embodied in their religion. Most were yeomen; none held large tracts of land. Many of the congregation bought and sold land regularly, usually among one another. (George Walker was typical of the community. Coming of age as a common laborer, he accumulated land. By the age of thirty—at the end of the 1720s—he had matured into a yeoman and a church leader.) Few economic distinctions or social differences beyond those of age and experience were obtained in Freehold. The great landowners of the area inherited their holdings and lived in Ireland or a more sophisticated part of the colony.

Many of the Freehold farmers were nearly illiterate, like Timothy Lloyd and Richard Watson, both of whom enthusiastically supported the passionate religion of the pietists. Few estate inventories contained books aside from the ever-present Bible. It was not necessary in Freehold to read or write well, since time for such activity was scarce. Joseph Morgan's attainments may have been admired by some, but they set him apart from his parishioners. Nevertheless, literacy did have some utility. The articulate, literate few became the county judges, and literacy could lead to a way out of the community for one's children. Robert Cumming, who sat among the elders of the church and helped sustain it with heavy contributions, would see his son—a small child during the Morgan controversy—become the minister of one of Boston's oldest and most prestigious churches.

Freehold, a former frontier community, was well on its way to settled agrarian status. It was not wealthy. No farmer had luxury goods to leave his family, and none left large estates. The most important household possessions were the rough tools of the farmer and the pewter ware and bedding of his wife. Most wealth was in terms of acreage and livestock. Very few—not even the leaders of the church—left more than 200 acres of land at their death. Despite its ethnic mixture, Freehold quite understandably supported only one minister. Thus, began the trouble, for the Dutch members of the congregation desired preaching in their own tongue and they invited Dominie Frelinghuysen for this purpose. But if the ethnic composition of the church began the divisions, it was not their ultimate basis. The spirit of pietism, not ethnicity, split the church after the arrival of Frelinghuysen and Tennent. Joseph Morgan was the victim.

Dissidence in the Freehold congregation was led by an English-speaking layman who considered himself as competent as his pastor. Walter Ker was a patriarch in his late seventies who had come from Scotland as a religious refugee. In the mother country he had been considered a "strict covenanter," one who took his religion seriously. Although the Ker family held a position on the subscription lists and seating charts of the church that clearly spoke for its importance, Walter was merely a "yeoman." In the period of Morgan's troubles, however, the old man sat in the front pew on the pastor's right, as befit a deacon of the church. Perhaps significantly, Ker's name did not appear among those who had originally installed Morgan, although he held a position of prominence in the community at that time.

The evangelical spirit of Frelinghuysen and the Tennents quickly produced a faction that was discontented with Morgan. It was probably led by men like Walter Ker who had long sought an issue. In any event, in 1728 the Synod of the Presbyterian Church, meeting in Philadelphia, examined seven charges brought against the Freehold minister by dissidents within his congregation. The complaints included "promiscuous dancing, intemperance, and the practice of astrology." Morgan's colleagues quickly dismissed the charges as unsubstantiated, and within a short time Morgan sat as moderator of the Synod. Clerical ranks had closed behind him, but the Freehold factionalists were unimpressed by their failure before the central authority of the church. Jacob Frelinghuysen had condemned Morgan for his formalism, and certainly the spontaneous religion of revival provided the settlers with a magical spirit of release and a strong sense of personal identity.

Apparently the Dutch dominie had a greater impact on the Freehold Reformed congregation than had at first been obvious. When Morgan withdrew, under increasing pressure from the pietists, the Classis of Amsterdam finally provided its charges in Freehold with a Dutch Reformed minister. But it was too late. To the great surprise of the Classis, the new minister found his congregation badly divided over the same issues that had split its English neighbors.

With Morgan's retreat, Walter Ker could seek the sort of minister the evangelical faction would appreciate—and one who would owe his place to Walter Ker. Quickly he rode off to Neshaminy to call a Tennent. John Tennent was brought to Freehold to harness the spirit of revival and the doctrine of the "new birth" left in Frelinghuysen's wake. However, in the face of deep divisions in the church, he seemed reluctant to accept the call. Freehold, Tennent said, seemed to be a community of people "whom God had given up." But once he reached the pulpit all opposition faded before the power of his appeal. Those who had scoffed at the new ways were silent. And many joined in the new reformation. "Tears were shed when he preached, while Frolicking, Dancing, Horseracing, with other profane meetings were broken up."

Young Tennent called for a rebirth, admonished the sinful nature of his parishioners, and damned those who opposed him. He was ordained November 19, 1730, at age twenty-three. Gilbert Tennent participated in the ordination, as did Jonathan Dickinson, who was developing a reputation as a leader of the moderately pietist Presbyterians. In the typical colonial fashion before 1740, when the clergy accepted the decision of a congregation as the will of God, Joseph Morgan also participated.

John Tennent preached evangelically for two years, and was warmly received by many as a "gracious blessing." Suddenly, however, this "most Successful, well Qualified and Pious Pastor . . . Departed this life"—on April 23, 1732. The congregation resigned itself to his death as "A Mournful Providence & cause of great Humiliation." But the evangelical movement now had greater substance than was offered by single personalities, and old William Tennent had more sons. John had always been delicate, and once had fallen into a long trance he later labeled as a mystical experience. William Jr., who was ordained at Freehold in late September 1732, was physically hardier. He could carry the revival in Freehold and the surrounding area through the Great Awakening. Indeed, Freehold became one of the bases from which the Tennents drew their strength and their support.

The Tennent-Frelinghuysen alliance brought the spirit of evangelicalism inherent in Protestantism to the surface through their preaching. Interacting across language and national barriers, which were particularly disruptive in the Middle Colonies, the universality of the evangelical search for personal salvation found expression in the classic cry from their pulpits: "What must I do to be saved?" Such preachers set aside the formal restraints offered by the refinements of logic and established tradition. They let the call echo in each breast as they looked down from their Calvinist pulpits. The early formula was terribly simple—perhaps insultingly so to those who reveled in unraveling the intricacies of theology.

The theme was repetitious. Man is a depraved sinner, destined to evil on earth and to damnation in eternity. He must search his soul to recognize his depravity, which, once it is seen, permits hope. Once the unequivocal evil of the sinning state is recognized, once the totality of depravity creates a sense of horror, the individual is prepared for a God-given rebirth. Here is the point of revival for eighteenth-century America. The reborn, who achieved that state through an indescribable and relatively formless internal experience, could anticipate the beauty of salvation in the future and appreciate the joy of harmony with God in the present. Every act could now be good and true. Life on earth could be dedicated to the glory of God.

Not surprisingly, the New Jersey revivals were accompanied by a profound concern for social behavior. The "awakened" demanded singular attention to religious matters. They damned all frivolous amusements as detracting from man's primary responsibilities. In some ways the austere code was reminiscent of the early Puritans. Now, however, the expected conduct included a more public display of one's purity than did the introspective Puritan code. Paradoxically, joyous celebration was not permitted to follow the intensely emotional experience of conversion. It seemed as if all natural needs for overt expression had been met by the spiritual experience. An exacting and restrained code of conduct for life could now be expected. At this stage of revivalism, therefore, there was no dancing in the streets. But there was a willingness to confront formalism, to divide congregations in the name of God's grace.

As the Tennents gained strength in the Middle Colonies during the 1730s, the mysterious spirit of God started working in Northampton, Massachusetts. Suddenly, and without obvious external cause, the backsliding and spiritual decline in the Northern community slowed and then stopped. The first signs appeared in 1732, when the young started attending public worship more regularly and with more sobriety. They seemed more willing to take advice. There had been no flood, no earthquake, no epidemic. Their pastor, Jonathan Edwards, observed a thorough reformation. New, private religious meetings were held among the young at his suggestion. The elder members of the community followed the example.

Edwards also detected a reaction against Arminianism, as the sense of religious concern continued to grow in the community. "And then it was, in the latter Part of December [1734], that the Spirit of God began extraordinarily to set in. . . . Suddenly five or six persons appeared savingly converted." One woman, who had been a notorious "company-keeper," impressed Edwards particularly. The call to conversion, he said, was a "Flash of Lightning, upon the Hearts of the young People." The revival continued through the spring and summer of 1735. "It was a time of Joy in Families on the Account of Salvations being brought to them"— although Edwards also admitted that some of these people neglected their worldly obligations. Most significantly, of course, the conversation and conduct of the people took on a more sober and religious tone.

The Northampton revival spread, first to South Hadley and Suffield, then to Sunderland and Deerfield. Edwards insisted that its growth was without human agency, through God's effort alone. But Edwards' presence in other parishes and the publicity the revival secured undoubtedly contributed to its extension. It moved to West Springfield, Longmeadow, and Enfield. Finally it moved through Connecticut to the parishes of Eleazer Williams at Guilford and Mansfield, and then to the eastern part of the colony. Even the congregation of the conservative and comfortable Reverend Joseph Noyes of New Haven experienced a small awakening. This was no small localized affair, and yet no obvious natural disasters were involved. Something new was clearly under way in New England.

Some clergy soon attempted to analyze the excitement. Most were sympathetic but cautious. William Williams of Hatfield, full of evangelical spirit, published a judicious call resting on the heritage of New England and the advantage of being religious. Peter Clark of Salem offered a full dissertation on the nature of conversion, calculated to win over the most cautious Calvinist. Eliphalet Adams of New London warned that at a time of awakening those who were saved should be particularly careful to avoid a "Deceitful work." He advised against false responses to calls for revival because the movement was spreading in the glare of publicity. After all, there were those who would "mock and Deride," and their hands could only be strengthened by a lack of caution. Edwards himself worried about those who saw the movement as a "distemper."

New England, like the Middle Colonies, had been preparing for revival for several decades. Pietism had spread. Evidence of awakening was abroad. In New England, where all religious matters were defined as paramount and gained a thorough airing by an exceptionally articulate elite, the ground seemed particularly fertile. Quick minds could build on the experience of others. But just what was meant by revival confused the scholarly leaders of New England once a large sample was offered in 1734. Few thoughtful Puritans doubted that God's providence was blessing His northern colonies, but what did it mean?

Edwards' own account of his revival, published in 1737, caught the proper tone. The clergy were God's agents, offering a word here, a call to meeting there, an occasional explanation of God's hand on the heart of a parishioner someplace else. Nevertheless, such a position was significantly different from denying human agency in the event. Any careful reader of Edwards' *Faithful Narrative* recognized that the Northampton pastor had been intimately involved in the expansion of the revival.

In the face of the excitement, theological orthodoxy must be guaranteed. After 1734, sermons were studded with assurances that doctrine had not changed and would not be altered. Watch for "Deceitful work," Eliphalet Adams had warned. Eleazer Williams, who had seen his parishioners through several small revivals, insisted that the carefully written word, in Scripture and clerical tracts, was God's primary tool. Samuel Moody of York made the same point. Cautious words must always have a prime place in a list of means to divine appointment. Most knowledgeable Puritan pastors, already battling with the latitudinarians, moved slowly but inexorably toward revival in the 1730s. With uneasy caution they repeated the clichés of orthodox theology, but they admitted that conversion could be preached.

By 1740 the American colonies were prepared for a major awakening. The Middle and Northern colonies had experienced successive samples of revival in response to a sympathetic shift of attitude which had been occurring for several decades. Even in the predominantly Anglican South, small enclaves of Calvinists turned toward the new pietistic notions coming from the Northern press. On the frontier, particularly in Georgia, German pietists were welcomed, and Anglicans of a pietist bent, like the Wesleys and Whitefield, were sent to serve the English population.

A great and general revival of religion might well have occurred in America in the 1740s even if George Whitefield had not made his appearance. But someone who could serve as a catalyst for the scattered developments was useful—if not essential. As we today are well aware, popular movements seem to have a life of their own. They build up slowly, almost clandestinely, and then move from their underground existence into the mainstream under the impetus of a charismatic, popular leader.

CHAPTER FIVE

The Course and Progress of the Great Awakening

*Three preachers in three distant places born,
Georgia, New Brunswick and Southhold did adorn,
The first to strike the passions did excell, The next
was famed for sending souls to Hell, The last had
nothing of his own to show, And therefore wisely
joined the former two.*

—*New York Weekly Journal*, July 12, 1742

For more than a generation colonial America had experienced scattered signs of the power and appeal of the doctrine of the "new birth," from Jonathan Edwards' Connecticut Valley revivals to the efforts of the Tennents in Pennsylvania and New Jersey. By the end of the 1730s, much of the colonial population was predisposed to respond to evangelical pietism. The Anglican itinerant, George Whitefield, tied all the diffuse threads together, turning isolated instances into a general phenomenon, the Great Awakening.

The revival which Whitefield sparked went through several identifiable phases in the years following 1739. Whitefield himself concentrated on major urban centers (mainly in the North) in his colonial tour of 1739 and 1740, and the Great Awakening began there. Soon other clergymen were emulating Whitefield's example. They spread the revival into smaller cities and the countryside, so that by 1742 most of the colonies north of Virginia were affected.

In both its earliest urban phases and its general extension, the revival met little serious opposition or open criticism, though questions cumulated in the minds of potential opponents. By 1743 the concentrated excitement was over in both the urban and rural communities of the Northern colonies. The course of the Awakening split in three directions. One was a bitter postmortem debate on its merits, mainly by the clergy and other intellectuals of New England. Another was a diffused continuation of a spiritual awakening in the South, particularly in Virginia. The third was an extension onto the frontier, largely by radical elements among those who had been revived, of individual versions of the principles of evangelicalism.

Whitefield and the Urban Revivals

George Whitefield was one of the most controversial figures of eighteenth-century Anglo-America. He is perhaps best appreciated today as an early manifestation of a hero of "pop" culture, and contemporary reactions to him have parallels in the responses engendered by Elvis Presley, the Beatles, or the Rolling Stones. Though Whitefield did not flaunt the private morality of his times, he certainly challenged the public.

His father died when George was a child, and he was raised by an indulgent mother, wife of an innkeeper. Exposed in his youth to the life of the tavern and its frequenters, as an adult he sternly disapproved of all aspects of that life. A bright and sensitive lad, Whitefield had a knack, which he never lost, of finding important patrons to further his career. He worked his way through Oxford as a servitor, bowing and scraping to the young gentleman scholars while privately excoriating their "extravagant living." At Oxford he met the Wesleys and became a "methodist." Finally, in 1735, his attempts at a satisfactory relationship with God were rewarded with a crisis conversion which for the remainder of his life served to verify the reality of the sudden experience of God's gracious love.

His conversion turned Whitefield to public prophesying, and thanks to a sympathetic bishop (for he was under age), he was ordained a deacon of the Anglican church. In 1736 he began public preaching across the country, provoking much uproar and widespread publicity. Refused admittance to most pulpits, he turned with great success to open-air preaching. By the time of his first trip to Georgia (in the wake of John Wesley's abortive sojourn there in 1737), Whitefield was a successful and notorious evangelist. In Georgia he found a lifelong goal: the building and maintenance of his famous Bethesda orphanage (raising funds for the orphanage was the ostensible reason for his first and subsequent American preaching tours). In 1738 Whitefield returned to England to take priest's orders. And in October 1739 he voyaged back to America to begin his most famous itinerancy.

In his first American tour, Whitefield characteristically moved rapidly from place to place, covering an enormous territory. Landing in the Lower Counties of Pennsylvania, he spent some weeks in the Pennsylvania–New Jersey area, and then went overland to Savannah, Georgia, preaching at every stop. He returned from Georgia to Pennsylvania by ship in April 1740, went from Philadelphia to New York City, back to Philadelphia, and then back to Savannah (this time mostly by sea) in May. The bulk of the summer was spent between Charleston and Savannah, but by mid-September he had disembarked at Newport, Rhode Island, to begin his controversial New England tour. Despite a two-week stopover in Boston, by the end of October Whitefield had traveled from Newport to New Hampshire, back to Boston and on to Northampton (where he met Jonathan Edwards), and then to New York City. He moved south to Maryland via Philadelphia, and returned to South Carolina by sea. Back in Savannah on December 13, 1740, Whitefield was aboard ship for England by mid-January of 1741. It had been a whirlwind tour, but somehow Whitefield found time to keep a daily account of his reception in the colonies, which was subsequently published.

From Whitefield's own accounts and those of his contemporaries, one point stands out: the bulk of his time was spent in Charleston, Philadelphia, New York, and Boston. Because of strong opposition in Charleston and New York, the visits in these two cities were somewhat marred and less than total successes. But Philadelphia and Boston were utter triumphs, both in terms of Whitefield's reception by important lay and clerical leaders and in the response of the general population. In Philadelphia he dined "with Mr. Penn, the proprietor, and prayed with and gave a word of exhortation to more than a roomful of people, who came . . . to hear the Gospel of Christ." In Boston, Governor Jonathan Belcher rode with him in the Governor's coach to public meetings. When the evangelist left the city, he "went with the Governor, in his coach, to Charlestown ferry, where he handed me into the boat, kissed me, and with tears bid me farewell."

In both cities, the bulk of the influential clergy welcomed Whitefield and opened their meeting houses to him. By all accounts, the crowds at his public sermons consistently numbered in the thousands. Through these successes Whitefield publicized—if he did not introduce—the basic ingredients of popular evangelicalism in colonial America. His own use of the ingredients could hardly be emulated, but others took what they could from his example.

One of the principal factors in Whitefield's success was advance publicity. As with most popular figures, the publicity was the result of a subtle combination of a natural and a studied image, of conscious strategy and unexpected windfalls. His success snowballed, and Whitefield knew how to exploit it. Any publicity was good publicity, since it made people curious. Even before his first appearance in America, he had acquired a considerable reputation as a successful evangelist. American newspapers reprinted reports of his activities by supporters and opponents, and Whitefield had already begun to add to the publicity by printing "journals" presenting his interpretation of what was happening. A visit in any area was always preceded by local publication of his journals and by newspaper accounts, often supplied by an agent dispatched in advance by the evangelist. Such publicity was obviously much easier to disseminate in large cities, which helps account for his principal impact on urban areas in America.

Equally important in explaining Whitefield's urban successes were his own psychological needs. Whitefield required huge crowds. He was a performer, perfecting his platform techniques, feeding the emotional needs of his audience with the sensitive shifts of an actor, but feeding *upon* them as well. It was not accidental that contemporaries frequently appraised the evangelist as they would a performer, and that some of his greatest admirers were popular actors such as David Garrick, who once exclaimed that he would give a hundred guineas to be able to pronounce "O!" as Whitefield did. From his childhood Whitefield had been fascinated by the stage, and when he gave up secular life he simply shifted his special talents into the religious arena.

Whitefield was clearly at his best when performing before a large audience, holding its attention with his histrionic abilities and his magnificent vocal modulation. "He had," according to Benjamin Franklin, "a loud and clear Voice, and articulated his Words and Sentences so perfectly that he might be heard and understood at a great Distance, especially as his Auditories, however numerous, observed the most exact Silence." Jonathan Edwards' wife, Sarah, observed:

> He is a born orator. You have already heard of his deep-toned, yet clear and melodious voice. It is wonderful to see what a spell he casts over an audience by proclaiming the simplest truths of the Bible. I have seen upwards of a thousand people hang on his words with breathless silence, broken only by an occasional half-suppressed sob.

Contemporaries were clearly impressed by Whitefield's ability to hold the attention of large crowds—much as they might be with a juggler's ability to keep several objects in the air simultaneously.

Met face to face, Whitefield was larger than life and somewhat overpowering; his eyes were huge and flashing and, judging from several surviving paintings, had a tendency to cross. But before a crowd, the effect was quite different. According to Nathan Cole of Connecticut:

> When I saw Mr. Whitefield come upon the scaffil he lookt almost angellical; a young slim slender youth before some thousands of people & with a bold undaunted countenance & my hearing how god was with him every where as he came along it solumnized my mind & put me in a trembling fear before he began to preach for he looked as if he was Cloathed with Authority from the great god.

As Cole's account suggests, a large part of Whitefield's appeal depended on the size of the audience he was manipulating. Although he could attract large numbers of listeners in any populated area, he was obviously drawn to the city because of the potential size of the audience. Cities brought out the best in Whitefield, and, like most performers, he had a considerable ego which needed constant reinforcement.

No other contemporary evangelist could match either Whitefield's publicity or his histrionic abilities. He was the master to whom all other excited evangelists turned for their lessons, and all learned something from him. Itinerancy became one of his most important style-setting contributions, emulated by his admirers and damned by his opponents. The very notion of constant travel, of preaching on the move, made each of his appearances a great theatrical occasion for the local community. Nathan Cole also described the crowd which gathered for Whitefield in the lower Connecticut River Valley:

> When we came within about half a mile of the road that comes down from hartford weathersfield & stepney to middeltown on high land i saw before me a Cloud or fog rising i first thought off

from the great river but as i came nearer the road i heard a noise something like a low rumbling thunder & i presently found it was the rumbling of horses feet & this Cloud was a Cloud of dust made by the running of horses feet . . . to carry his rider to hear the news from heaven for the saving of their Souls. . . . i found a vacance between two horses to Slip in my hors & my wife said law our cloaths will be all spoiled see how they look for they was so covered with dust that they looked allmost all of a coler.

In Whitefield's hands, itinerancy was very much like a personal appearance tour by one of today's pop music aggregations.

Itinerancy had some real advantages for the evangelist. It permitted him to preach ex tempore without boring an audience. Of course, the sermons were not made up on the spot; rather, they were so frequently given that no notes were necessary. As Franklin said of Whitefield:

His Delivery . . . was so improv'd by frequent Repetitions, that every Accent, every Emphasis, every Modulation of Voice, was so perfectly well turn'd and well plac'd, that without being interested in the Subject, one could not help being pleas'd with the Discourse, a Pleasure of much the same kind with that receiv'd from an excellent Piece of Musick.

Like most performers, Whitefield had a limited range. His sermons consisted basically of several dramatic variations on a single theme.

Settled parish ministers, who had lived with their flocks for years and had instructed them in the ethical and moral values of Christianity, operated at a considerable disadvantage when compared to the itinerant. Their preaching lacked novelty, and by 1740 most had unfortunately fallen into the habit of reading their complex exhortations from their pulpits. Preaching without notes was not only an innovation in the colonies, but it permitted—indeed required—the evangelist to emphasize emtions and feelings rather than carefully developed intellectual systems. Constant movement provided fresh audiences for the specific emotional appeal, and it avoided discovery by the audience of the lack of variation.

For Whitefield and most of his imitators, itinerancy tended to obscure the restricted intellectual context of evangelicalism. George Whitefield was no theologian. But neither he nor most of his listeners was bothered by the relatively thin doctrinal content of his sermons. Indeed, by simplifying doctrine and focusing attention on one aspect of spiritual life—the conversion experience —Whitefield was able to make a popular appeal which cut across denominational lines, socio-economic divisions, and geography. According to Whitefield, the essential truth of religion was the "new birth." He dramatized the eternal disasters lurking for those who did not find their way to Christ while emphasizing the joys for those in his audience who did:

> O believers! (for this discourse is intended in a special manner for you) lift up your heads; "Rejoice in the Lord always; again I say, rejoice." Christ is made to you of God's righteousness, what then should you fear? You are made the righteousness of God in him; you may be called "The Lord our righteousness." Of what then should you be afraid? What shall separate you henceforward from the love of Christ? Shall tribulation, or distress, or persecution, or famine, or nakedness, or peril, or sword? No: I am persuaded, neither death, nor life, nor angels, nor principalities, nor powers, nor things present, nor things to come, nor heighth, nor depth, nor any other creature, shall be able to separate you from the love of God, which is in Christ Jesus our Lord, who of God is made unto you righteousness.

Slashing through all the complicated theological controversies of the time, Whitefield's goal was a simple one—to lead his listeners to be "born again."

The theological debate over whether conversion was an instantaneous or gradual process was a very old one among those who emphasized the need for conversion. Most Protestants, and especially the Calvinists who were dominant in North America, could agree on the steps or stages of conversion: Christian knowledge, based upon church attendance, family worship, and catechism; "conviction," a perception of the helpless and hopeless condition of the individual; grace, a will and desire to believe in and accept

God; combat against doubt; and, finally, some personal confidence of God's grace. The debate occurred, at one point, over the necessary relationship between a lengthy period of Christian knowledge, conviction, and grace. It focused, at another point, on the need for another lengthy period between the initial infusion of grace and its final certainty. Whitefield and his fellow evangelists concentrated on foreshortening the period between conviction and final confidence, usually by blurring and condensing the steps around a sudden and complete experience of grace. Whitefield himself had had a sudden conversion, and he never doubted that the new birth could or should occur in such a manner.

By its very nature, the evangelical concentration on a sudden new birth appealed to individuals beset with strong inner tensions and desperately in need of resolution. The insecure and anxious were to be found everywhere, of course, but young people on the verge of maturity, their future unclear, their present wants and desires frequently in advance of their material and emotional resources, were particularly susceptible. Consider some of the trials which one night beset Hermon Husband of Virginia when he was about eighteen years old. In a hurry to return to his lodging house to pray, he met a woman on the path. "It was not so dark," he wrote, "but I saw her some Distance, and Satan suggested instantly in my Mind, assisted by the Lust of the Flesh also, as ready to take Hold of the Woman as she pass'd me, but yet nothing immodest." Husband wrestled with his temptation for a minute, and then "pass'd the Woman by, and neither touch'd nor spoke to her." His experience made him "presently ashamed, especially when I remembered how great a Hurry I had been in, but how I had slack'd my Pace to consult with the Flesh and the Devil, nor could I not pray for Shame and Confusion of Face." Other young people recorded similar experiences.

The operational assumptions of the evangelist were basically little different from those of modern popularized psychiatry, and particularly such therapy techniques as "encounter groups." If people have tensions and anxieties, they also have a craving for quick release from the pressures of such emotional afflictions. As in encounter therapy or other shock techniques, the evangelist sought to exploit the individual's need for a cure. If the individual's tensions and anxieties can be heightened to the point where he is virtually overwhelmed by them, where he feels completely helpless (the evangelists called this "conviction"), something is likely to happen. At the point of helplessness, which is usually brought about or accompanied by strong feelings of guilt, the modern therapist introduces an integrated program of insights and rules which both "explain" the individual's problems and provide guidelines for behavior so as to avoid them in future. The patient feels better because he believes he has been given answers, and if the original difficulties were not deep seated, he probably will be "cured."

The evangelist pursued a strategy similar to that of the therapist. With guilt and anxiety heightened to the point of helplessness, the preacher could offer an individual new birth and salvation as the solution. Nathan Cole described the release:

Now I had for some years a bitter prejudice against three scornful men that had wronged me, but now all that was gone away Clear, and my Soul longed for them and loved them; there was nothing that was sinfull that could any wise abide the presence of God; And all the Air was love, now I saw that every thing that was sin fled from the presence of God. As far as darkness is gone from light or beams of the Sun for where ever the Sun can be seen clear there is no Darkness. . . . Now I saw with new eyes, all things became new, A new God; new thoughts and new heart.

Colonial Americans were always potentially responsive to evangelical therapy, but only around 1740 did they begin to get it in dramatic form.

Despite his own perhaps inflated sense of personal achievement in bringing Christ to America, George Whitefield recognized the advantages to be gained by allying himself with favorably disposed local clergymen wherever he was preaching. He had no hesitancy about preaching in dissenting churches, if the ministers would make a pulpit available, and usually he appeared publicly with local ministers. In New York City, for example, a Dutch critic complained that

Domine Dubois, and Domine Frelinghuysen (the latter having allowed Mr. Whitefield to preach to his congregation at Raritan), and the dissenting minister here went in company with Mr. Whitefield out of the city of New York, into the open fields, to hear him preach. They also went up with him on the stage erected for him, and sat down behind him.

In the Pennsylvania–New Jersey area, Whitefield traveled in company with Gilbert Tennent, the latter deferring to the Anglican's obvious charisma and learning a good deal about evangelical techniques in the process. In Boston, Whitefield exploited his support by many local clerics and politicians in every way possible.

By such actions, Whitefield identified himself with well-known local ministers and clearly demonstrated his ecumenicalism. Although leaders of his own Anglican church objected strenuously to Whitefield's connections with dissenters, this only strengthened his appeal to non-Anglicans. But as Whitefield benefited from ecumenicalism, so did those willing to join him. Connection with Whitefield identified a minister with the man and movement of the hour, and many clergymen who had tried or who sought to be evangelical could observe at close hand a master at work.

Whitefield's first tour of America was a signal triumph, but it was not devoid of criticism and opposition. He encountered objections, though both the nature of his calling and his personal attitude toward opposition turned the criticism to his advantage. Much of the articulate early opposition came from within his own Anglican church, particularly from Commissary Alexander Garden of Charleston. Whitefield's widely publicized feud with Garden, culminating in July 1740 with an attempt by Garden to try Whitefield in his ecclesiastical court for breaking canonical vows, only increased the evangelist's popularity with the vast majority of colonials, who already were hostile to the Anglican establishment in America.

While Whitefield's cries of persecution in the Garden case were particularly appealing to the non-Anglican majority, complaints of harassment whenever he encountered opposition were always effective with those who prided themselves on a sense of fair play. Whitefield's injured innocence whenever he was criticized was not simply a pose; he sincerely believed that, since his was Christ's cause, such attacks were made on the Savior Himself. The mantle of self-righteousness which Whitefield wrapped about him only goaded his critics into further opposition. Whitefield's evangelical followers shared his sense of crusading self-righteousness and mission. Such beliefs not only protected the revivalists from insecurity and self-doubt but infuriated opponents into overreactions which obscured their legitimate objections.

By the time of his return to England in early 1741, George Whitefield had instigated the American Great Awakening. In some regions and with some individuals, his preaching tour was mainly a spur to activity. This was particularly true of Gilbert Tennent and the Presbyterian revival in the New Jersey–Pennsylvania area. In other cases, however, Whitefield opened new possibilities and showed how to translate them into action.

If Whitefield's American tour laid the groundwork for the evangelical successes of the early 1740s, it also contained the seeds of the controversy which would ultimately overwhelm the revival. Not many colonials in 1740 recognized their inherent opposition to what Whitefield was doing, and most of those who did held their tongue. But Whitefield and some of his successors would, over the next few years, push the evangelical position to its extreme limits. In 1741 most Americans—certainly most colonial clergymen —were prepared to accept and experiment with evangelicalism as a strategy for reviving the spiritual mission of the New World. But most were neither prepared to make evangelicalism a way of life nor to insist that it was the only strategy.

Extension into Rural Communities

Well before Whitefield's tour was completed, others had joined him on the evangelical trail. Gilbert Tennent had long been "itinerating" in the Middle Colonies, but in the summer of 1740 he moved into south Jersey and Maryland, with some success. Soon after, he met Whitefield in New Brunswick, and at this conference Tennent agreed to accept invitations to visit New England; he arrived in Boston in October 1740. He was an entirely different preacher from Whitefield. Where the Englishman concentrated on the beauties of God's love, Tennent focused on the terrors of damnation—delivered not at all mellifluously. The New Brunswick pastor had a loud, high-pitched voice, which at its deepest could be criticized as "beastly braying" and at its shrillest degenerated to a nasal whine that frequently was imitated by others. But Tennent was sincere, experienced, and militant. He had for years been battling traditionalistic elements within his own Presbyterian church over discipline, education, and especially itinerant preaching.

On March 8, 1740, Gilbert Tennent delivered a sermon in Nottingham, Pennsylvania, which castigated most of the ministers of his region (and, by implication, throughout America) as unconverted men. They were compared to the Pharisees and labeled "subtle selfish Hypocrites" who were "wont to be scar'd about their Credit, and their Kingdom; and truly they are both little worth, for all the Bustle they make about them." Such men were opposers of God's work, "Swarms of Locusts, the Crowds of Pharisees, that have as *covetously* as *cruelly,* crept into the Ministry, in this adulterous generation." Tennent maintained that "it is both lawful and expedient to go from them to hear Godly Persons." Reports of Tennent's position and his successes preceded him in New England, and thus many came to listen, perhaps hoping to hear their own clergy condemned.

Gilbert Tennent had long been preaching revival, and the reception accorded Whitefield merely emboldened him to widen his horizons and declare open war on the traditionalists. But Whitefield also galvanized previously sedentary and silent ministers into action. Men like Eleazer Wheelock, pastor of an obscure Connecticut parish, began successful preaching tours. Wheelock started in eastern Connecticut in mid-October 1740 and preached his way through Rhode Island and southeastern Massachusetts to Boston, keeping a journal, Whitefield style, of his activities: "Preached at 10. A great outcry in the Assembly. Many greatly wounded." In Taunton, Massachusetts, he noted: "I believed 30 cried out: almost all the negroes in the town. . . . Colonel Leonard's negro in such distress that it took 3 men to hold him. I was forced to break off my Sermon before I had done, the outcry was so great.'' Such were the satisfactions of the revival trail.

The preaching tours of Tennent and Wheelock signaled a second phase of the American revival, which began late in 1740. Where Whitefield had concentrated upon preaching in major communities, spending most of his time in the large urban centers, the Tennents and Wheelocks were willing to preach to smaller communities off the major postroads of the Northern colonies. They, in turn, encouraged local pastors to preach evangelically, either in their own or in neighboring parishes. In chain reaction, Whitefield's successes in places like Philadelphia and Boston spread into the hinterlands of New England and the Middle Colonies.

As we have seen, rural pastors had a variety of spiritual and secular reasons for responding favorably to evangelicalism. Most of them in 1740 felt threatened, and many had long been sincerely convinced of the spiritual deadness and growing secularization of their congregations. Accounts of their local revivals, published between 1743 and 1745 in Thomas Prince Jr.'s *Christian History,* almost invariably began with a statement of pre-revival conditions—like that of Nathaniel Leonard of Plymouth's First Church:

> Religion was then under a great decay; most people seemed to be taken up principally about the world and the lusts of this life; though there appeared some serious Christians among us that had the things of God at heart, who greatly bewailed the growth of impiety, profaneness, and other evils, which threatened to bear down all that is good and sacred before them. We were sensible of an awful degeneracy, and kept days of fasting and prayer, year after year, that God would pour out his Spirit upon us; especially on the rising generation.

Implicit in this concern over the declining state of spirituality was an understandable clerical anxiety over the status of the minister in his community. This was particularly true in New England, where clergymen hearkened back to the golden age of early settlement, when pastors had led their communities, but it was also true of many Presbyterian ministers in the Middle Colonies.

Pastors found that they and their churches were no longer dominating forces in their communities but merely one of a number of competing factors. Worse still, in churches like those in New England and their Presbyterian cousins of the Middle Colonies, which continued to insist upon a learned and reasonably paid ministry and high standards of belief and behavior for church membership, declining membership—relative to the churchgoing population at large—meant that the "unregenerate" (those who did not exhibit the standards) were footing the bills. In New England particularly, where public ecclesiastical taxation was still a reality, the minister came into conflict with his roles as shepherd of his flock and as a public employee of the community.

In the years before the revival, clergymen had responded to new threats in a variety of ways. Some had adjusted to the new situation by lowering the standards of church membership or ceasing to attempt to act as moral policeman for the community; others asserted strong personalities which dominated their communities despite the problems. Such ministers tended to be relatively unresponsive to evangelicalism. They were the "Pharisees" against whom Gilbert Tennent inveighed in his Nottingham sermon, or the traditionalist "Opposers" so common in New England. Most pastors, however, were caught between their inability to surrender to the new secularizing conditions or to dominate through force of personality. They had attempted to regenerate religion through tried-and-true techniques. They had used every natural disaster as an excuse for a sermon warning their congregations of insufficient piety. They had fought politically to close the taverns; they called fast days and pleaded with their people. New England pastors had special problems with the practice known as the halfway covenant, which permitted the children of church members (and eventually all their descendants) to gain a kind of associate membership in the church. Many New Englanders found this sufficient, while others entertained a concept of the exclusiveness of full membership well beyond any insistence by their pastors on traditional spiritual standards.

Most clergymen did not consciously embrace evangelicalism as an innovation. They considered their support of the Awakening to be essentially conservative, in maintenance of existing doctrine and church practices. The techniques of mass evangelism popularized by Whitefield may have been relatively new to colonial America, but they could be fitted within traditional doctrine and could be employed apart from the daily operations of the church. Revivalism was embraced by most ministers because it served to quicken the spiritual interests and concerns of the population, who were thus encouraged—hopefully without altering the standards of church membership, local ecclesiastical practice, or theology—to become serious Christians and active church members.

Unfortunately, most responsive pastors (usually called New Lights in New England or New Sides in the Middle Colonies) were caught between extremist church members, who sought to alter the existing ecclesiastical arrangements consistent with their own experiences of the new birth, and the opponents of evangelicalism who became concerned with what they considered abuses of the techniques of revivalism. In the mind and practice of most clergymen, revival preachers were imported as an external agency to "quicken" the population, while long-standing local standards of membership, baptism, and church discipline were invariably retained. Opponents of the Awakening doubted that the status quo had been maintained. They pointed out that after 1740 men joined churches following sudden experiences, and that the latter attacked settled ministers for not going far enough. Many ministers who encouraged revival tried to treat matters such as the nature of conversion and itinerancy as "nonessentials," but others did not agree. The posture of preserving tradition by supporting nonessential innovation has always been difficult to maintain, particularly since not everyone agrees on essentials. But such a purpose lay at the heart of much clerical support for the Great Awakening in the early 1740s.

By the beginning of 1741 the revival had spread far beyond the centers which had responded so enthusiastically to Whitefield. In the Middle Colonies, at least fifteen Presbyterian ministers were itinerating, chiefly in New Jersey and Pennsylvania, and numbers of German pietists also were active. In New England, over 100 ordained clergymen were preaching for conversions in their own and neighboring parishes, and they were joined by several dozen young men, typically university graduates who lacked settled parishes, in traveling about the countryside. For the most part, New Light preachers remained in their own regions and preached in a parish only upon invitation of the incumbent minister. Only a handful of men, after gaining publicity and notoriety, established evangelical reputations which transcended their own counties.

Revival preachers whose contemporary reputations were at all widespread—men like Benjamin Pomeroy, Andrew Crosswell, Nathanael Rogers, Eleazer Wheelock, and especially James Davenport—were the exception rather than the rule. Most of colonial America's rural Awakening was accomplished without great fanfare (except for subsequent reports in the revival periodical *The Christian History*) by individuals who had no reputation as successful evangelists. Usually the pastor led his flock to various levels of evangelical excitement with only the aid of an itinerant's brief visit and stories of activity elsewhere.

Peaks of revival activity were reached at different times in different areas during the years 1739 to 1745. The Middle Colonies, thanks to the activities of Gilbert Tennent and others who preceded Whitefield's tour, probably peaked earliest, perhaps by mid-1740. The first half of 1741 was the high point of excitement in Boston, its suburbs, and most of Connecticut. The farther a community was from Whitefield's preaching orbit (away from the major lines of transportation, communication, and commerce in the colonies), the later the revival hit. Much of southeastern Massachusetts and especially Cape Cod, for example, did not "awaken" until late in 1741 and early in 1742. The northern counties of Massachusetts (now Maine) and New Hampshire stirred only in 1742. The edges of the major internal routes of the seaboard colonies, such as the eastern counties of Virginia, were not aroused until 1744 and 1745, when Middle Colony Presbyterians brought evangelicalism into the Upper South. Like most popular movements, the Great Awakening began in the urban centers and filtered into the hinterlands in concentric rings along established channels of communication.

As the revival spread, its supporters gained confidence and its opponents amassed evidence of excesses. At the beginning of Whitefield's tour, only a handful of colonials spoke out in opposition to the practices of evangelicalism. Most Americans, including the clergy, desired a spiritual reawakening and hoped fervently that the popular responses evoked by Whitefield and his successors would provide it. As the revival grew and its implications unfolded, many discovered that they were not willing to pay the price. From an initial position of hopeful optimism, large numbers of colonials began to move slowly in opposite directions.

A pattern of polarization (familiar to modern Americans) gradually developed. Many evangelicals who were active in spreading the revival occasionally passed beyond the bounds of consensus; a few almost defiantly passed beyond them. Some began to push evangelicalism to its extreme, logical conclusions, and others seized upon the excesses as a reason to limit the spread of the movement. Opposition, increasingly expressed in newspapers and pamphlets but more meaningfully through governing bodies in church and state, led to struggles with alliances of evangelicals for control of those bodies. In some cases, opposition provoked evangelical defiance of ecclesiastical and secular authority. Excesses were met with attempts at repression, which produced further excesses, which produced further repression. Eventually almost everybody lost sight of the original issues.

There were issues aplenty. A wide variety of evangelical assumptions and actions posed potential threats to ecclesiastical stability and the status quo, particularly as interpreted by many ordained ministers of important colonial denominations, such as the Presbyterians and Congregationalists. Evangelical itinerancy and censoriousness were related menaces. Gilbert Tennent's Nottingham sermon, charging that most of his fellow clergymen were unconverted, is a clear illustration of censoriousness. And George Whitefield dismayed even his heartiest supporters when the published journal of his New England tour commented of Yale and Harvard that "their Light is become Darkness, Darkness that may be felt, and is complained of by the most godly Ministers." Many graduates of those institutions felt personally attacked.

Beyond feeling directly challenged by charges that they did not "experimentally know Christ," clergymen realized that the logica extension of the criticism was to justify following some preacher who did; Tennent's Nottingham sermon had concluded with just this point. Equally abhorrent to many ministers and laymen were the emotional and physical responses of listeners to the evangelists. Descriptions of the audience reactions were published not only by those unsympathetic to the movement but also by the itinerants and their supporters. People cried out, writhed in agony, collapsed, sang, and generally behaved in abnormal ways. Even such a staid evangelist as Jonathan Parsons was deeply moved by the response to such a sermon:

> Many had their countenances changed; their thoughts seemed to trouble them, so that the joints of their loins were loosed, and their knees smote one against another. Great numbers cried out aloud in the anguish of their souls. Several stout men fell as though a cannon had been discharged, and a ball had made its way through their hearts. Some young women were thrown into hysteric fits. The sight and noise of lamentations seemed a little resemblance of what we may imagine will be when the great Judge pronounces the tremendous sentence of "Go, ye cursed, into everlasting fire." There were so many in distress, that I could not get a particular knowledge of the special reasons, at that time, only as I heard them crying, "Woe is me! What must I do?" And such sort of short sentences with bitter accents.

All previous excesses were outdone by James Davenport, pastor of the Southhold, Long Island, Church. Converted by Whitefield and Tennent in Philadelphia in 1740, Davenport in the summer of 1741 crossed Long Island Sound to Connecticut to begin a controversial career as an evangelist. What Davenport did most successfully was publicize and dramatize the dangers of evangelicalism when carried to its most extreme conclusions. He ultimately was brought to recognize this fact himself, and apologized for his activities, but in his heyday Davenport knew few bounds. Unlike Whitefield or Tennent, who preached extemporaneously but with order and calculation, Davenport "had no Text nor Bible visable, no Doctrine, uses, nor Improvement nor anything Else that was Regular."

It was impossible to distinguish between his sermon and his prayer, and he was likely to burst into song at any moment. Joshua Hempstead of New London described a Davenport sermon: "He Calld the people to Sing a New Song &c forevermore 30 or 40 times Immediately following as far as one word could follow after another 30 or 40 times or more & then Something Else & then over with it again." Worse still, Davenport cultivated the habit of dropping in unannounced at the home of the local clergymen to examine the state of their souls. And he usually found that clerical souls were unconverted, a discovery he would announce in his next public sermon. Furthermore, he encouraged those in his audience who had "seen the light" to become itinerant preachers, whether or not they had theological training and clerical approval.

Davenport's antics reached their height in New London early in 1743, when he induced an audience to burn "sundry good and useful treatises, books of practical godliness, the works of able divines," as well as "hoop petticoats, silk gowns, short cloaks, cambrick caps, red heeled shoes, fans, necklaces, gloves, and other such apparell." While psalms and hymns were sung over the pile, the preacher added his own pants, "a pair of old, wore out, plush breeches." This, commented one critic, would have obliged him "to strutt about bare-arsed" had not the fire been extinguished. Even before the New London escapade, however, clerical ranks (including most New Lights) had closed against Davenport—but not before he had contributed to a widening rift in colonial opinion.

The Debate over the Awakening

If 1739 and 1740 had seen only scattered criticism of the spreading revival, opposition began to mount in 1741. In Boston, the co-pastor of the venerable First Church, Charles Chauncy, published his first open attack on the Awakening. Mr. Chauncy was a rational man of regular habits. An old friend described his daily routine: "At twelve o'clock, he took one pinch of snuff, and only one in twenty-four hours. At one o'clock, he dined on one dish of plain wholesome food, and after dinner took one glass of wine, and one pipe of tobacco, and only one in twenty-four hours." Perhaps not surprisingly, Chauncy was repelled by sermons which struck at men's bowels, and he quickly became the revival's leading opponent.

In western New England, Jonathan Edwards, sensing a growing hostility to revivalism, desperately attempted to distinguish between its positive and negative aspect. In a sermon titled *The Distinguishing Marks of a Work of the Spirit of God*, Edwards defended the Awakening despite emotional excesses of which he quite openly disapproved.

But the major event of 1741 was the open schism in the Presbyterian Synod of Philadelphia. Divisions had long been apparent among the Presbyterians, and particularly between the native-born and -educated ministers, led by the Scots-Irish Tennent family (who sought a relaxation of rigid rules and standards and decentralization of authority in the church), and Scots-born and -educated pastors, who refused to adjust the organization and assumptions of the church to colonial conditions, particularly the rapid spread of settlement. The revival catalyzed the opposing factions and precipitated a break. Unable to alter the existing structure from within, the Tennents and their supporters (all proponents of the revival) left the Philadelphia Synod and formed their own New Brunswick Presbytery in the heart of the "awakened" countryside of New Jersey.

In 1742 opposition to the Awakening accelerated. Chauncy alone published four anti-revival tracts, and the number of attacks in books and newspapers was extensive. Perhaps more menacing, the Connecticut Assembly in May of 1742 passed "An Act for regulating Abuses and correcting Disorders in Ecclesiastical Affairs," which included strong penalties for uninvited itinerancy and lay preaching, and required all ministers to be licensed by local ministerial associations. Connecticut had long been noted for strict state control of religion. The Saybrook Platform of 1708 had granted ministerial associations more power to enforce conformity than was available in any other American colony. But the legislative action of 1742 was still a warning to supporters of the revival that the bounds of conformity and consensus had been exceeded.

A month later, James Davenport and Benjamin Pomeroy were arrested and tried before the Connecticut Assembly. Pomeroy, whose "demeanour tho' by itself wild and extravagant, yet comparing with the other gentleman, seeming almost orderly and regular," was dismissed. But Davenport was declared insane and unceremoniously escorted to the borders of the colony. Not surprisingly, the pro-revival clergymen of Boston quickly joined in the general condemnation of Davenport's "disorders and that Prophaneness which have been promoted by any who have lately gone forth to hear him"—a desperate attempt to disassociate the revival from his activities. Even Gilbert Tennent publicly stated his "Abhorence" of Davenport, which was reinforced by troubles the Presbyterian leader was having in his own bailiwick with competition from radical lay exhorters, such as the Moravians.

By 1743 supporters of the revival were under attack on many fronts. Charles Chauncy, after several years of collecting every piece of evidence of evangelical abuse conceivable, put it all together in his monumental *Seasonable Thoughts on the State of Religion in New-England*. Eleazer Wheelock later bitterly commented: "I was upon that same road to N. Haven when that Dr. passed through this government (as I understand) to fill his crop with materials for that piece and I came several times within the scent of him (for he left a savour of what he fed upon when he lit)." But neither Wheelock nor anyone else, including Jonathan Edwards, could deny that Chauncy had collected an enormous and damning catalogue of documentable excess.

Even before the publication of *Seasonable Thoughts* the Massachusetts Ministerial Convention, meeting in May in Boston, had blasted "several Errors in Doctrine and Disorders in Practice, which have of late obtained in various Parts of the Land." Supporters of the revival called their own convention for July, which could do no better than declare that "there has been a happy and remarkable revival of religion in many parts of this land, through an uncommon divine influence," in a testimony which proceeded to admit and warn against "many irregularities and extravagances" which "have been permitted to accompany it." In 1743 the Lutheran Synod of America split similarly over the issue of the revival.

The basic fact was that all settled clergymen—whether New Lights or Old Lights—were threatened by the fanaticism of those who had been converted. By 1743, ministers in most areas of the

Northern colonies no longer could bask in the excitement of large increases in membership and the reformation of morals. Instead, they found themselves under attack by some of their parishioners for not going far enough and by others for going too far.

If conversion was necessary for church membership, and was as emotionally sudden as it had been during the revival, what about those who had become members before the Awakening? Were they truly converted? If all converted men were equal in God's eyes, and if grace were the only mark of a true Christian, then why all the clerical emphasis on professional standards such as education and formal ordination? If all Christians were equal, all could exhort and preach the Gospel. And if any converted soul could preach, why did ministers insist on being so well paid for their activities? Prevailing practices such as the halfway covenant in New England came under attack, and some individuals began to ask how infants could be baptized if grace (which supposedly requires some intellectual assent) is the distinguishing mark of a true Christian.

All over America, clergymen discovered that the revival, instead of uniting pastor and flock in spiritual assent, brought a new wave of lay criticism of the churches. Years of unrest with ministerial authority and church practices came to the surface, and the more committed not only criticized their churches but left them when satisfactory changes were not made. In the Middle Colonies, such malcontents frequently joined German pietist sects such as the Moravians. In New England, a new denomination gradually emerged from the extremist separations, based on the new birth, democratic church organization, hyperzealous missionary activity, unpaid ministers (who needed no formal education), and believer's baptism. This denomination, usually called Separate Baptist, met with only limited success in settled portions of New England. But its zeal, organization, and program were ideally suited for missionary activity in newly settled back-country regions everywhere in America.

Back-Country Revivals

By 1743 the Great Awakening was dying in the urban and settled regions of colonial America. Only the South had yet to be affected. The Tidewater area of Virginia was reached by Presbyterian missionary activity only in the mid-1740s, and the back-country South would wait a generation longer. After 1743 the major impact of revivalism was in the back country, on the frontier—always the most difficult area for organized religion. (University-educated ministers hesitated to risk their careers on the uncertainty of the wilderness; settlements were small and widely scattered; money was in short supply.) Even before 1740 a few missionaries had been active in the back country, but the revival provided a veritable army of men with the commitment and the beliefs to succeed under frontier conditions. Because the frontier was constantly moving, always expanding in colonial America, evangelical activities were constantly expanding to keep pace with settlement.

Even arch-opposer Charles Chauncy had seen the possibilities of frontier evangelism. In 1744 he had semifacetiously asked the Massachusetts Ministerial Convention:

And are there not vast Numbers in the neighboring Governments of VIRGINIA AND NORTH-CAROLINA (not to say any Thing of the Natives) who live almost in heathenish Darkness? And would it not discover as much Love to Souls, and as disinterested Zeal to serve the Redeemer's Kingdom, for Ministers to travel up and down, preaching the Gospel to these People, as to go about from Place to Place, where the Gospel is preached every Sabbath-Day, and Person call'd to the Work, qualified for it, and fixed in it? *There* is Room for *itinerating:* and the more abundant any are in it, the greater will be their Glory: Nor will any one be dispos'd to withhold from them the Praise that is their Just Due.

Chauncy recognized the suitability of evangelicalism for the frontier, but he also demonstrated the sophisticated urban dweller's disdain for rural life. He did not understand the vast potential of the back country.

Separate Baptists, and to a lesser extent Presbyterians, reached the same conclusions as Chauncy, though for more positive reasons. Their subsequent activities were less a revival—in the sense of the Awakening of the early 1740s—than the introduction of regular religion into areas previously lacking that amenity. No complicated psycho-social explanation is needed to explain the success of the frontier evangelists: they succeeded because they came. Preaching a simple doctrine of the new birth and organizing democratically structured churches aided their reception by frontiersmen, but Anglican missionaries did equally well in the back country when they made the effort. The Great Awakening provided the personnel and the program, and the back country was an empty vessel into which they could be poured.

The Presbyterians moved from Virginia into the Carolina and Georgia back country in the 1750s, and were soon followed by itinerant Separate Baptists, particularly Shubael Stearns and Daniel Marshall, both Connecticut men who had been converted in the Great Awakening. About the same time, the New England Separate Baptists, led by Isaac Backus, another Connecticut convert, began evangelical activities on the northern frontier in New Hampshire and those regions which eventually became Vermont and Maine. By the time of the American Revolution, even Nova Scotia was being visited by New England itinerants.

In one sense, therefore, the Great Awakening never stopped. The thrust of evangelical pietism on the frontier continued to thrive so long as there was a frontier. But in another sense the Great Awakening *did* end, degenerating into a nasty and bitter quarrel over its meaning among those who had been most intimately involved.

CHAPTER SIX

Intellectual Factions of the Awakening

Does not the spiritual Man judge all Things? Tho' he cannot know the states of subtil Hypocrites infalliby; yet may he not give a near Guess, who are the Sons of Sceva, by their Manner of Praying, Preaching, and Living? Many Pharisee-Teachers have got a long fine String of Prayer by Heart, so that they are never at a Loss about it; their Prayers and Preachings are generally of a Length, and both as dead as a Stone, and without all Savour. I beseech you, my dear Brethren, to consider, That there is no Probability of your getting Good, by the Ministry of Pharisees.

—Gilbert Tennent, *The Danger of an Unconverted Ministry, Considered in a Sermon . . . Preached at Nottingham, in Pennsylvania, March 8, Anno 1739, 40*

The revival quickly became a cause of confusion, a symbol of disorder, and the catalyst for religious change and new factional divisions throughout the American colonies. To attempt to categorize the position of men in the course of the Great Awakening is filled with hazard. As in any complex movement, men of all shadings of conviction could be found. Moreover, they did not remain perfectly consistent either over time or over the wide spectrum of issues the revival unleashed. Some, like Joseph Morgan of New Jersey, could move in the course of the Awakening from opposition to support. Some, like Charles Chauncy of Boston, could shift in the face of social disruption from qualified support to ardent opposition. Others, like Gilbert Tennent, could remain committed to the revival while becoming increasingly concerned about its excesses. Individuals were forced to shift their views in both overt and subtle ways, as the experience of the Awakening gave them new insights into the implications of the movement. Dogmatic consistency was to be found, but this was hardly typical.

However fluid they were, some meaningful factional lines emerged in the America of the Great Awakening. Perhaps the lines were clearest in New England—always the intellectual center of religion in the colonies—but they could be observed everywhere. Because of the complexities of men's views, it has always been possible to convert subtle differences into a great multiplicity of positions. But in the last analysis, only three constantly shifting factions are worth distinguishing. Traditionally, the division has been made into pro-revivalists (called New Lights or New Sides) and anti-revivalists (labeled Old Lights or Old Sides). Although the opposition to the Awakening was amorphous and motivated by varying factors, it had a certain unity in its negative critique. But among the revival's supporters there was a critical division into two wings, which can be labeled "moderate" and "radical." In general, the moderates accepted the innovations of the revival in order to preserve the essentials of the existing religion and society as they perceived them. The radicals, on the other hand, were more willing to follow the implications of the revival in whatever direction they led, even if this meant a fundamental reordering of tradition. The radicals of the Awakening, limited by their era's cultural assumptions, were not typically concerned with the sorts of issues which today mark the radical, but in their own time they were viewed with suspicion and fear by moderates and conservatives alike as destroyers of the fabric of society. For the sake of analysis, it is perhaps best to begin with the centralist position, that of the moderates.

The Moderates

By at least a third of the clergy of New England and the Middle Colonies, the Awakening was greeted with excitement and delight. It appeared as a providential reply to twenty years of complaint against the religious deterioration of the Northern colonies. And, seemingly, it called for no sharp break in theological profession. The essentials of revival lay in the tradition of piety which had been developed over the previous decades. Men who saw the revival as the logical outgrowth of the past were the moderates of the Awakening. Many of them had already been preaching the necessity of a "new heart," the central core of pietism always inherent in Puritanism in both its Presbyterian and Congregational forms. Now the evangelicalism of revival gave such men new, loud, unqualified, self-conscious support for their actions.

The evangelical emphasis appeared in George Whitefield's first Boston sermon, *Tree of the Heart Is by Original Sin Exceedingly Corrupt and Thus Being Made Good by Regeneration*. Whitefield held, as had Jonathan Edwards ten years earlier in Boston, that salvation could come through Christ alone. As also was the case with Edwards, the point of such emphasis was neither the Calvinist insistence upon man's utter dependence upon the will of God for his salvation nor a cry for a "knowledge" of Christ. Instead, Whitefield, Edwards, and most of the moderate advocates of revival reasserted the covenant of grace as an avenue to a conversion experience. The rhetoric of revival seemed to imply a return to the harsh, uncompromising doctrines of Calvin, with their emphasis on election for a few. But in fact, by loosening the bonds of preparation for salvation and by emphasizing one's sense of ecstatic joy as evidence of election, the moderates opened salvation to thousands who had been unable to experience it through the more rational, dispassionate processes of the past. "New birth" or a "new heart," rather than "old sin," was the issue at stake from the beginning of the revival.

America had never heard religion presented in such a passionate fashion from its traditional pastors. Many of the scholarly Puritan leaders of Boston found George Whitefield's incautious use of language slightly disturbing, but so long as he remained reasonably vague in his detailed consideration of doctrine, the clergy could ascribe his exuberance to the imprudence of his extraordinary youth. Whitefield could be accepted and enjoyed for his emotionalism and, above all, for his stimulation of popular religious excitement. To confirm Whitefield's place as a part of old, orthodox Puritanism, the respected Thomas Prince—co-pastor of the Old South Church—insisted that Whitefield preached the "doctrines of the martyrs and other reformers, which were the same our forefathers brought over hither."

The change of heart that followed from a religious experience had always been part of Puritan doctrine and constituted nothing new in its religious life. For the moderates, this assertion that the simplistic nature of revival was in conformity with the teachings of earlier generations represented the essence of their position. Over and over, the moderate supporters of the Awakening insisted on the orthodoxy of their adherence to the ways of revival. Over and over, they insisted that the excitement of the revival could be described as God's providential blessings on the community. Regularly the leaders called for adherence to the standards of the past and rejection of unnecessary innovation. Always they cautioned against the hazards of Arminianism on the one hand and Antinomianism on the other. They never hesitated to restrain and oppose excess.

None asserted this sense of continuity between the revival and long-held religious tradition with greater constancy than Thomas Prince. The Old South pastor sought to make the revival appear as little more than God's expansion of Christianity. Even Cotton Mather, years before, had said that there was too little of Christ in the sermons of many ministers. Prince himself had been warning for years against those who would see too little of God in normal events. Edwards, as early as 1731, had sharpened the issue of

God's omnipotence by insisting on God's absolute sovereignty in salvation. The revival seemed simply to direct the proper attention to religious matters, for which men like Prince and Edwards had been crying for many years. With the revival in full blossom, Prince exclaimed that "this work of grace is God's pouring out of His holy spirit among a people." Its wonder came not from its newness but from its volume. God still acted as a "spirit of grace, and this is in both ordinary and extraordinary degrees in manners in the same or several ages, according to his sovereign pleasure."

For the moderates, in an elaborate series of sermons, Prince established a continuity for the Awakening as part of God's regular providence. He appropriately turned to Christian history to make his point, utilizing a periodization that clung to a traditional insistence on the uniqueness of New England. The first sermon covered the years 1517 to 1630, ending with the settlement of New England. Starting with both Luther and Calvin as examples of revival, Prince came quickly to the persecution that brought "the most zealous" of the reformers to the "Indian thickets." Another sermon brought the events of "pious" history down to the present period. The following sermons were devoted to the current revival. The result was a huge collection of scriptural evidence to guarantee the authenticity of the Awakening as God's providential act, illustrating that it was nothing new and explaining the process of what Jonathan Edwards called "visible conversions." Prince insisted that Scripture showed man's natural impotence for—even aversion to—a voluntary change of heart. Hence, he concluded, it must be a work beyond the power of men.

The great statements of the orthodoxy of the moderate position came in 1742 and 1743, as the strength of the movement began to wane and its leaders became defensive. Jonathan Edwards and Thomas Prince, the chief moderates of the New England revival, harmonized their concerns in two publications. In 1741 Edwards had produced *The Distinguishing Marks*. Then, as excitement and confusion surrounding the revival grew in 1742, he extended his analysis in *Some Thoughts Concerning the Present Revival of Religion in New England*. Edwards intended this tract as instruction for New England in the proper conduct of revival, hoping to resolve some of the confusion manifest in the community. In orthodox fashion he granted the importance of reasoning and of understanding doctrine, and hinted that some had neglected this. He then warned against accepting false evidence of religious experience, suggesting that, after viewing the revival, he could discern a certain "uniformity" in its operation and insisting that it conformed to the scriptural picture of true religion. Edwards also adhered to the orthodox belief that God's ways are inscrutable, beyond knowing. Thus the individual could never be certain of his state. Accordingly, argued Edwards, the religious experience of others could not be judged by mortals.

In his conclusion, Edwards suggested that a history of the progress of the revival should be published once a month or once a fortnight by one of the Boston ministers who was close to the press and the main channels of colonial communication. "It has been found by experience," he wrote, "that the tidings of remarkable effects of the power and grace of God in any place, tend greatly to awaken and engage the minds of persons, and other places." To this point Thomas Prince responded with the *Christian History, Containing the Accounts of the Propagation and Revival of Religion*. The first issue appeared March 5, 1743, only a few months after Edwards' recommendation. The title page carried the name Thomas Prince Jr. as editor, but no one in the community doubted that the father was the determining force behind the issue.

For a periodical, *Christian History* had amazing unity and logical development during its span of publication. The work as a whole provided a context for the Great Awakening by connecting it with past events and the tradition of New England's founders. An enormous array of information portrayed the revival as consistent with traditional Puritanism. Prince appealed to the authority of New England's early settlers and to the movement's universality in the Protestant world as evidence of its nature and vitality. As the Awakening lost its force, the *Christian History* succumbed to growing criticism. But it stands as a grand testimony of the moderates to the orthodoxy of the revival.

Unlike George Whitefield, who fastened onto the conversion experience without analysis, the moderates felt compelled to understand and explain the process. If they were to defend their insistence upon orthodoxy, they were forced to demand a period of preparation for conversion on the part of those who responded to the cries of the evangelists. Preparation for conversion had always been a critical part of the Puritan tradition. It had been a major force in restraining the natural inclination of Puritan orthodoxy toward evangelicalism. All the moderates defended the need for a describable process of conversion, and most of them hurried on to offer a specific explanation of what this process entailed. Preparation had to be somewhat deemphasized because of its affinity to logical proceduralism, which compromised God's omnipotence.

Jonathan Dickinson, the leading moderate of the Middle Colonies and a powerful Presbyterian leader, called for "steps" to a sense of sin and misery, then an awareness of human, natural impotence, and finally a genuine knowledge and acceptance of God's saving ways as preparation toward ultimate conversion. Thomas Prince saw the process as a deep awareness of sin, sufficiently profound to excite the sinner to seek God, then a sense of faith, and ultimately a developing holy bent, combined with an illumination that brought a deeper hatred of sin and a vision of the beauty of holiness. Finally came the actual experience of conversion. Dickinson and Prince were in general agreement on both the nature and context of the preparation procedure. The Presbyterian presented his argument as a mental exercise in self-consciousness, however, while Prince directed his emphasis toward the emotional emptying of one's soul to make it a proper receptacle to be filled with the light of God's grace.

The final word on conversion came from Jonathan Edwards in 1746 with the publication of the *Treatise Concerning Religious Affections*. A logical extension of his *Thoughts* of 1742, the *Treatise* was the last writing of Edwards to deal specifically with the revival. In 1746 the Northampton pastor insisted at great length that there was no particular order or method of operations and experiences in the process of conversion. This abandonment of the sequential process was a sharp departure from tradition, and opened opportunities for a variety of religious experiences that were particularly compatible with evangelism. Instead of developmental stages, Edwards emphasized a number of signs that would always accompany true religious experience. The signs, however, offered little help to the individual in his practical search for regeneration. For Edwards, conversion could be known only after it had been achieved, and then only by the individual affected. In place of the stages of the old order, the twelve signs of Edwards were qualitative results of a total change of heart, an absolute acceptance of the truth of religion.

Jonathan Edwards was always too introspective and intellectual to be neatly labeled, but his ultimate rejection of the traditional stages of conversion illustrates some of the difficulties inherent in the moderate position. The endless self-conscious assertion by the moderates that their support of revival constituted nothing theologically or religiously new tells more about their values than about their actions and ideas. The position was a defensive one. Hardly social revolutionaries who could be accused of seeking reorganization of either the religious or the secular community, the moderates represented an establishment that had been losing ground for several generations. To their minds, the revival offered an opportunity for reassertion of their traditional roles as community leaders. Awakening seemed to point toward an increase of spiritual concern among the people that could only enhance the position of their spiritual leaders, the clergy. The moderates wished to return to the old, and most of them perhaps never recognized the amount of innovation they were willing to introduce to move backward. Even Edwards, with all his genius, refused to see the inconsistencies. His congregation recognized innovation when they saw it, however, and no amount of subtle distinction between means and ends could dissuade them from ultimately dismissing Edwards from his pulpit when he tried to change the rules. However defensive the position of the moderates became, support of revival represented some critical shifts in the way in which religious experience was approached and perceived.

Intellectually, the moderate position represented a sophisticated acceptance of the changed climate for the ideas of the Age of Enlightenment. In the larger sense, the Newtonian cosmos had replaced older, more cumbersome formulations of the universe, and many of the moderates had absorbed this thinking for at least a generation. In a more specific sense, the reasoning of John Locke was most influential. Locke's views on epistemology and the freedom of the will yielded a new dimension to religious experience that American intellectuals like Jonathan Edwards, Thomas Prince, and Jonathan Dickinson would find extremely compelling. The singleness or wholeness of mind, spirit, and emotion which followed from Locke's statements on the nature of ideation was crucial. While at first glance it may appear ironic that the most advanced colonial thinkers should have been moderates, this is not really so unusual. Defending "the system" by synthesizing the old and the new has long been a motivating force for major intellectual figures.

The singular role of Jonathan Edwards in understanding and absorbing the new intellectual mood established by Newton and Locke has been exaggerated. Apart from the human will, a Puritan belief in the unity of mind and body had in fact appeared in the medical views of the colonial intelligentsia as early as the 1720s. Cotton Mather, in his final, brilliant, unpublished work, "The Angel of Bethesda," had wedded mind to body as interacting forces in medicine. Following Mather, Thomas Prince could speculate during the Awakening on the role of the nervous system as the "immediate seat of the soul." Most of the intellectual leaders among the clergy had at least read the commentaries upon Locke, and could frame their arguments accordingly.

Writing well before Jonathan Edwards, Jonathan Dickinson had published a long scholarly work, *True Scripture Doctrine,* which developed an argument in thoroughly Lockean terms. Like all divines from the Calvinist side of the Reformation who clung to the essential doctrines of that persuasion, Dickinson sought to reply to those latitudinarians whose insistence on freedom of the will was labeled Arminianism. This was an address to the central problem of the age. Dickinson, writing in 1741, said that he could not "but think (with Mr. Locke) that it is a very inaccurate and obscure way of speaking, to attribute freedom or want of freedom to the will." He then developed the essentials of Locke's argument on the will, using this argument to defend religious orthodoxy in America in a way which anticipated Jonathan Edwards. Thomas Foxcroft, a Boston defender of the revival, wrote the preface for Dickinson's production, quite obviously understanding the point of his Middle Colony colleague.

In private correspondence, Foxcroft himself developed some

sophisticated notions about the nature of the will which harmonized with the spirit of Locke. In 1743 he engaged in an exchange of letters with Experience Mayhew, a missionary to the
Indians and an opponent of revival, discussing the views of Dickinson. A Lockean description of will, a defense of determination
in terms of that description, a view of the unity of understanding
and affection, and a dedication to experiential religion achieved
through the senses were ideas shared by many of the more sophisticated thinkers of moderate persuasion.

The implications of these ideas for revival reached final development with Jonathan Edwards, who attacked the Awakening's opposition for its distinction between reasonable and emotional religion. Such a distinction, declared Edwards, was both
muddled and false. Mind, heart, soul, reason, and emotion could
not be separated into categories, could not be compartmentalized.
God may make such strong impressions on the mind as to affect the
body, Edwards argued.

To make the confusion worse, the opponents of revival attempted to categorize affection and will. For Edwards, affections constituted a heartfelt response to experience and might be true or
false, depending upon their nature. An individual wills according
to his loves and hates, and these loves and hates are functions of
the affections: "The informing of the understanding is all vain, any
further than it *affects* the heart; or which is the same thing, has
influence on the *Affections*." Regeneration, Edwards made clear,
affected the total self and all its parts. A sense of wholeness lent
itself perfectly to the evangelical concern for a change of heart that
would involve an alteration of the very nature of the individual.
Above all, the source of knowledge and understanding had
changed under the impact of Locke's empiricism. Knowledge
came through sensual experience, and the vocabulary of revival
quickly absorbed the language of Locke in continual assertions
about senses and responses.

The moderate advocates of revival delighted in the new
techniques offered them by the chief itinerant clergy for exciting
congregations and communities to the new religious interests.
Many of them, as carefully trained scholars, found religious revival easily compatible with the intellectual moods of the Age of

Enlightenment. But with a single voice and tremendous determination, all insisted upon the essential orthodoxy of their position and all explained the movement only in quantitative terms. It was *more*, not *different*. Had there been no other view in support of revival, the moderates might have remade American Protestantism with little drama and great ease. Unfortunately, at least from the moderate standpoint, the Great Awakening brought forth men of many persuasions, some of whom took a far different position in support of revival. Popular movements have a tendency to get out of the control of their intellectual leaders. Careful thinkers like Jonathan Edwards or Jonathan Dickinson were hardly representative spokesmen for the Great Awakening.

The Radicals

Radical revivalists offered the most dramatic dimensions of the Great Awakening and the issues for most of the rhetoric in the enormous quantity of printed matter arising from the movement. The moderates found themselves either trying to harmonize their views with the radicals or, more frequently, disavowing their association with them, while the radicals largely ignored the moderates' distress and delightedly permitted the implications of the Great Awakening to lead where they would. Generally, the radicals were more ready to accept the implications of social disruption inherent in the excitement of revival. They tended to adhere less to notions of "ancestor worship" and more to theological innovation than did the moderate advocates of the Awakening.

They were, in the first place, ardent advocates of itinerant preaching under all circumstances. Secondly, the radicals attacked the ordered religious establishments by insisting that unconverted ministers occupied many of the colonial pulpits and by denying that these unconverted clergy could contribute to the salvation of their congregations. Finally, radical supporters of revival generally accepted the "doctrine of assurance," the concept that one can know with some certainty his place among the elect and that certain knowledge of one's election in itself constitutes critical evidence of a satisfactory conversion experience.

At the height of the Great Awakening, in the years between 1740 and 1743, the line between moderate and radical supporters of the revival was particularly hard to draw. Indeed, it frequently came down to the extent of one's involvement in the daily demands of revivalism. The more engaged a man was in the actual process of extending the Awakening, the more radically he would act and speak. Most clergymen of established religious denominations, however, gradually became disenchanted with the excesses and errors of the revival—particularly among the newly converted laity. By the mid-1740s the older churches contained only moderates and opponents. Radicalism was forced outside the establishment, flourishing among schismatic groups like the Separates and Separate Baptists of New England and sectarian groups like the German pietists of the Middle Colonies. During the revival's heyday, almost anyone might have been a radical.

Evangelical itinerancy was one of the key issues. In establishing a model for itinerancy, George Whitefield unintentionally set up the objections to it. For many, he and his successors, who would preach wherever an audience could be gathered, came to symbolize the militant attack on the establishment perceived by the revival's opponents. When these itinerant evangelists combined their rambling travels with an attack on the unconverted local clergy, the lines of battle were unequivocally drawn (James Davenport's case was only the most visible example of such confrontation). For many colonial clerics, opposition to itinerancy was desperately defensive. The itinerant challenged not only the local clergyman's right to lead his congregation but his very right to preach.

By long tradition, the entire American religious community had not only permitted but encouraged occasional clerical visitors who might offer a local congregation new insights into Scripture or imaginative admonitions against the neglect of religious duties. Such pastoral visitations had always been carefully controlled, however. A visiting preacher appeared only upon invitation from the regularly established pastor. Moreover, he traveled from his own parish, where he held a legitimate pulpit. Evangelical itinerancy began in the New World with at least a gesture to these accepted standards, but itinerancy soon provided the most dramatic dimension of the Great Awakening. It served as the issue around which much of the printed debate revolved.

Uninvited preaching within the territory of a minister proved to be a critical problem. Eleazer Wheelock's correspondence was studded with defensive comments on his preaching without proper invitation. Daniel Bliss wrote excitedly to Wheelock that the ministers—wherever he went—hated him. He had just preached in a town "where the minister had by no means consented thereto," and he was now moving on. Wherever an itinerant appeared, he drew heavily from regular congregations for his audience. But even more critical, and in large measure underlying the fervent attacks against itinerancy leveled by the regularly established clergy, were the charges brought against these clergy by some itinerants. "He taxes with great freedom," the New York *Gazette* said of Whitefield's sermons in that city, "the vices and errors of the modern clergy; and they in return generally hate him." Here were grounds for open conflict. The evangelists, with varying degrees of intensity, engendered the hate of their established counterparts by attacking them as ineffective, unconverted, sinful men. Indeed, the early comments of Whitefield were mild compared to the disruptive and unequivocal attacks upon the established clergy by some of those who followed in his footsteps.

Behind the freewheeling accusations of the radical itinerants was their conviction that many of the regular clergy were unconverted and thus harmful to their parishioners' chances for salvation. Gilbert Tennent's famous 1740 pronouncement of the danger of an unconverted ministry set the general tone for the radical position. The work proved important enough to appear in print in 1742, although Tennent himself had doubts about the social effects of his assertions before the end of 1743, having moved to a moderate position. Tennent said, simply enough, that "natural man" could not work with success for God's glory, for men who have no faith cannot be faithful. Certainly this appeared sensible, but problems arose in identifying unconverted ministers. Tennent avoided a precise formula, but he hinted very strongly at tests when he suggested that the "natural man" would not teach the doctrines of original sin, justification by faith alone, and other sound Calvinist points of view.

Most outspoken in his published attacks on unconverted

ministers—and one of the outstanding examples of the radical position—was Andrew Crosswell, a graduate of Yale. Almost alone among the major radical spokesmen, he supported the wild activities of the notorious James Davenport. In his 1742 defense of Davenport, Crosswell unequivocally declared the right to challenge the religious state of a fellow clergyman. In the spirit of Tennent's Nottingham sermon, he insisted that an unconverted minister could not know the way to heaven. Such a minister, knowing only the "wrong" way to approach God, could offer only the road to hell. Then, with more boldness than Tennent, Crosswell tried to tell how to identify the unregenerate. As Tennent had indicated, doctrinal purity offered one test, but Crosswell insisted that neither soundness in faith nor sobriety in life was sufficient. In addition, a clearly articulated experience of conversion was necessary. Without such an experience, the individual was unconverted. Crosswell, moreover, did not hesitate to attack the moderate advocates of revival. He described their position as "the way of the devil," arguing that such "sweet" religion was Satan transformed into the Angel of Light.

For three years the itinerants moved about the country, pursuing exhaustive schedules that had them preaching daily and sometimes several times a day. Crosswell called the preachers the men "God has own'd," and led the radical itinerants in justifying their roving practices as those of Christ Himself. Unlike many of the moderate revivalists, the radicals were not distressed by evidence that both their admonitions against unconverted ministers and their irregular techniques were socially disruptive. Crosswell, who had more intellectual power than most, spoke for the radical wing of the movement in 1742 when he accepted the charge of disorder. "The truth is," he wrote, "God never works powerfully, but men cry out disorder; for God's order differs vastly from their nice and delicate apprehension of Him." Using such an argument, the radicals were free to move as they pleased, even when charged with being disturbing itinerants and destructive separatists. Ebenezer Frothingham, a separatist leader, carried Crosswell's dicta one step further when he called for bold innovation regardless of its effect on the establishment.

The radicals' accusations against the established clergy were based upon their demands for an identifiable conversion experience and their confidence that such an experience was a valid awakening that assuredly placed the individual among the elect. This position was an important part of the radicals' intellectual pyramid. In conformity with Calvinist tradition and the moderates, the radicals insisted upon the conversion experience. Again like the moderates, they emphasized this identifiable experience as the core of individual religious involvement. But the radicals rejected cautious written accounts of the experience, and they went beyond both the moderates and the Calvinist tradition in their insistence that such an experience could be recognized as certainly placing one among the elect. From the belief in assurance of election came the notion that the state of others could be identified. Upon this conviction rested their confident condemnations of those ministers whom they labeled unconverted.

For the radicals, the fundamental problem was the nature and the certainty of conversion. These issues, which had plagued the Protestant world since the Reformation, stimulated new interest in the years immediately preceding the Awakening. As George Whitefield was making his first tour of the colonies, Daniel Wadsworth of Hartford traveled to a nearby community to visit with his colleagues for "much talk about Conversion, and how far and what an unconverted man can and what he cannot do; but with what darkness and confusion do we talk of these things." The radicals felt, as the revival gained momentum, that the darkness and confusion had been dispelled. Above all, they insisted upon a simple, categorical distinction between saved and not saved. To claim that the unsaved, "depraved" man in the state of nature could do nothing for God's glory was old Calvinist doctrine. But for the radicals, the logical consistency of their categorical distinction was expressed through their adherence to the doctrine of assurance. To their minds, the intensity of the conversion experience and the ability to describe it gave one proportional conviction and assurance that he was saved.

The doctrine of assurance had been present in one form or another in Christian thought since the Middle Ages. It was also one of the most difficult psychological problems facing Christianity, particularly after advocates of the Reformation had rebelled against the old forms and emphasized the individual personality and its relationship with God. Essentially, the doctrine of assurance met the problem of the need to derive comfort from belief and from adherence to the principles of religion. If the individual insists that only part of the population can be among the elect, then the problem of recognizing his or her position among those chosen few becomes critical. Election for the Calvinists, as for the advocates of revival, depended upon the infusion of grace through the conversion experience. But how does one determine whether the experience is true? Is the evidence of election to be found among the external appearances of the individual's conduct in society, or is it primarily an inner, spiritual experience?

At one end of the spectrum of experience leading to conversion was awareness of one's utter depravity and complete dependence upon God to overcome that depravity. How could the intensity of that conviction be sufficiently lessened to permit the beauty of conversion to be felt? For Calvin, the "spirit of adoption" gave the saints' enjoyment of their election a meaning which was "in some measure communicated to them." Such words offered comfort, but Calvin warned that those who "pry into the eternal council of God" run a risk of entering a "fatal abyss" should they go beyond the limits of God's word. The orthodox position asserted the likelihood of degrees of assurance, which depended (in social terms) on the evidence offered by one's conduct in the community and (in personal terms) on the endless process of self-examination to determine the state of one's soul. Real certainty was impossible.

The Great Awakening placed overwhelming emphasis on the conversion experience and brought a new intensity of emotion in the search of that experience. Inevitably, such emphasis and intensity rekindled interest in the doctrine of assurance. Old tracts were republished. Cautious clergymen reexamined, with great care and scholarship, the evidence for election. Jonathan Dickinson spelled out the problem precisely in a 1742 sermon: "What Security Can We Obtain That We May Safely Depend Upon, in This State of Darkness and Ignorance, Temptation, and Imperfection?" Dickinson first hedged his consideration against charges of a "doctrine of works" by pointing to the utter dependence of men upon God for their evidence. He found evidence in conduct and self-examination, and then turned to the critical issue: "Is Certainty Always Present and Is It a Necessary Tradition of Adoption?" In short, must one *continue* to live in an intense experience, wondering about the validity of his "adoption"? Could one not finally gain the comfort, the happiness, and the joy that come from unequivocable confidence in one's inclusion among the elect?

Dickinson asserted that "it is impossible . . . for any person at any age of observation to be ignorant of his conviction," but he maintained an orthodox position by insisting that assurances were not necessary for conversion. In conclusion, he made his evangelical concerns particularly clear by an emotional appeal to his congregation to avoid "dreadful uncertainty" and to seek the comfort of assurance as a final step in the individual search for salvation.

Among the radicals, led by Andrew Crosswell, the equivocation of Dickinson disappeared. In 1742 the line between the radicals and the moderates was clearly drawn, as the moderate leaders in New England attacked the radicals in a long publication in the form of a dialogue. The moderates specifically denied the doctrine of assurance, reasserting the Calvinist conviction that one could not be certain. Crosswell led the radicals in reply: "It seems to me," he said, "on the contrary the greatest absurdity in the world to suppose that the soul should trust Jesus Christ for salvation, and love Him and not be sensible of it."

Part of the issue, of course, was the nature of the evidence to be used in support of one's conversion experience. Moderates were held to insist that only outward evidence, or evidence gained through observation of the subject, could be used. Crosswell and those who supported the radical position damned such a view as a doctrine of works. They insisted upon the validity of the individual's testimony of his inward experience.

A year later, Samuel Finley, who would become President of the College of New Jersey (Princeton), expanded the doctrine of assurance with particular clarity and special regard for its implications and complexities. He did not hold, he said, that all true Christians are always assured of their "gracious" state. But, he asked, may not one "who is judicious and experimentally acquainted with things of the spirit of God know whether another be also acquainted with them?'' Finley, a graduate of the Log College, had attempted to maintain orthodoxy by suggesting that salvation could be obtained without assurance. But the real hazard of his words lay in the assertion that one who is in a state of grace may possibly judge the grace of another. At this juncture the doctrine of assurance had new importance for the radical revivalists, for through the confidence of assurance one gained the right to judge the state of others.

Finley continued down the narrow, possibly heretical path between traditional doctrine and innovative interpretation. Assurance, he explained, might be transient or fixed, and he insisted that even Christians who live mostly in darkness have their "lucid intervals" with "sweet, refreshing, and satisfactory inclinations of God's love." But upon this comfortably orthodox assertion Finley based the next dangerous position of radicalism. Those who lack a fixed assurance, he said, must be suffering from a "weakness of faith." Assurance could be felt in direct ratio to the strength of one's faith. For those of strong faith, assurance would be a firm "persuasion and satisfaction of a Christian about the safety of his soul, as wholly excludes all uneasy jealousies, doubts, and fears."

The radicals moved dangerously close to the "inner light" of Count Zinzendorf and the Quakers. They were in harmony with the thought pursued by John Wesley in the mother country. Those who stressed assurance could unearth many historical sources in Calvinist literature to defend their position. So long as they left room for election—for those who felt insecure—the literature was abundant. But the most useful source proved to be Samuel Lee's treatise of the late seventeenth century. (Lee had lived briefly in the New World, settling in Rhode Island and returning to England following the success of the Puritan Revolution.) His *Joy of Faith*, often used as a work of science, was a long, passionate treatise which emphasized the evangelist's call for a change of heart and the consequent doctrine of assurance.

With very careful, formal logic Lee argued the case for assurance by drawing the old distinction between universals (God's proclamations to the world in all ages) and particulars (God's promises to every believer in all ages). Assurance for the individual believer followed from a God of love Who extends mercy as the fruit of that love. Assurance of salvation, moreover, was instantaneous, a kind of irradiation within the soul of the saint. By definition, Lee insistedn assurance is the persuasion of our hearts concerning the love of God, producing in the saint a profound belief in his own faith. Because it was drawn from a personal application of the more general promise of God to the individual, Lee also called it "special faith." "But will God pardon me in particular?" he asked. "I answer I doubt it." Each is commanded, individually, to believe.

The writings of Andrew Crosswell reflected a reading of Lee, but Samuel Finley inadvertently revealed the peculiarly radical use of the doctrine when he answered a series of complaints against radicalism. He placed a defense of assurance next to the practice of charging ministers as unconverted. For the radicals of the Awakening, these two issues belonged together. By juxtaposing the two questions the radicals converted the extremely personal question of one's assurance into the social question of determining the validity of one's religious position within the community. Not only could one be certain of his own state, he could use that certainty as the basis for judging the state of others in authoritative terms. And these others might well be the leaders of the community.

Through the doctrine of assurance the radicals had reasserted the power of personal judgment, but then they took another giant step and claimed the right to pass judgment on others. The subtle ambiguities of classical Christianity, which had kept man in a state of uncertainty, were stripped away. A bold confidence in judging the fate of individual men was not only permitted but encouraged. Finley had rhetorically asked: "May not one who is . . experimentally acquainted with things of the spirit of God . . . know whether another be also acquainted with them?" The judgment could be carried out simply through conversation. Although the more cautious radicals would not claim infallibility for such judgments, this qualification did not nullify the social implication of the practice. It seemed to follow that one who failed to declare a convincing conversion experience was, indeed, unconverted. The clergyman, who daily exposed to others his understanding of God's way, was of course most vulnerable.

The doctrine of assurance could never be acceptable to the

moderates, particularly with its corollary of the right of the assured to judge the state of others. As one moderate advocate of the Awakening expressed it, "who can wonder, in such times as this, [that] Satan should intermingle himself to hinder and blemish a work so directly contrary to the interests of his own kingdom?" For the most part, the moderates ignored the doctrine of assurance and concentrated their attacks against the radicals on the issue of public judgment. But Jonathan Edwards, as he set forth the distinguishing marks of revival, said that one cannot know who is saved. Edwards was prepared to allow the individual the right of self-inspection, but he was not willing to expose potential saints to the scrutiny of others.

One of the most moving passages in Puritan literature is the soul-searching experience of Thomas Prince's daughter on her deathbed, seeking enough assurance to die without fear. She could not be certain of her salvation and her father could not offer such assurance. The traditional insistence on the inability to know with certainty one's place among the elect runs throughout the works of the moderates, echoing the religious thinking of generations of Protestants. To the moderates, nothing in the Great Awakening was new.

Radical and moderate supporters of the revival could agree in mutual acceptance of what seemed to be a broadly based expansion of religious concern. In general, the differences between the two groups of supporters of revival focused upon the self-conscious assertions of orthodoxy on the part of the moderates and the pretentious lack of concern for tradition on the part of the radicals. The two factions disagreed with one another frequently, both in print and in the churches. They could unite only in support of the Awakening as a work of God when it came under attack by the opposition. And in the enormous paper warfare between proponents and opponents of the revival, the moderates were the losers, trapped between consistent and defensible positions. Neither radical nor opponent accepted compromise. Critics of the Awakening refused to distinguish between the careful statements of the moderates and the disruptive actions of the radicals. Like the radicals, the opponents would not accept moderate revivalism as the orthodox position of sweet reason, which the moderates so vehemently insisted it was.

The Opposition

Not all American religious denominations had the same response to the Awakening. Some denominations, like the Quakers and Northern Anglicans, were almost to a man opposed to evangelical pietism and revivalism. Others, like some of the German pietist sects, merged almost imperceptibly into the revival movement. But for many denominations, particularly the New England Congregationalists, the Middle Colony Presbyterians, and the Southern Anglicans, the revival brought division, with some of the most articulate members of the religious community leading the opposition. Both Harvard and Yale remained in the control of the Awakening's opponents, and the powerful religious establishment in Connecticut had sufficient strength to legislate against itinerancy. In the Middle Colonies, the young Presbyterian Synod split over the revival, with each side hurling passionate and vitriolic thunderbolts at the other. In the South, the clergy of the Church of England scoffed at evangelical doctrine and battled against itinerancy, while thousands of their parishioners were enchanted by the preaching of the evangelists. Other denominations—but only after the concentrated outburst of religious enthusiasm and public debate had ended—would reap the benefit of revival in the South.

In all regions of America there was hostility to the Awakening from its outset, although in 1740 few clergy were willing to state their opposition publicly, and even fewer clergy, at any point in time, were prepared to refuse the gains in membership which came from the increased emphasis upon religion which the revival produced. As the religious and secular communities gained experience with revivalism, however, opposition to its excesses grew substantially. In Boston in 1740, George Whitefield was warmly and excitedly greeted. When he returned in 1745, all America had known four years of debate over the merits and demerits of revivalism, and he was subjected to considerable abuse.

The opponents of revival cried out against the heresy of responding to what they called "secret impulses" as the rule of conduct, in place of strict attention to the written word. The reliance of the radicals on "secret impulses" was a particular embarrassment to the moderates. The moderates always insisted on the use of the written word as part of the process of conversion, while the radical itinerants had been most eager to abandon the intellectual standards of the past and reap the harvest of sudden impulse. Opponents also insisted, as did the moderates, that one could not have the certainty of conversion, that sanctification was evidence of justification, and that those who believed otherwise were guilty of "antinomian familistical errors which flow from these."

Heading the list of practical errors lamented by opponents of revival was itinerancy, "by which either ordained ministers or young candidates go from place to place, and without the knowledge, or contrary to leave of the . . . pastors in such places, assemble their people to hear themselves preach." This, of course, was the heart of the revival, and without itinerating there could have been little hope of continuing the Awakening. Critics further protested "private persons of no education" who set up as preachers, for such persons invaded the sanctified ministerial office and represented a destructive force to authority in the churches. Some criticized those who separated from established churches to follow "lay exhorters or itinerants," and others attacked those "persons assuming to themselves the prerogatives of God, to look into and judge the hearts of their neighbors, censor and condemn their brethren, especially their ministers." On many of these issues the moderates suffered from an arbitrary identification with the radicals, which contributed significantly to the growing opposition to the revival.

To one degree or another, nearly all the opponents complained bitterly of the wild antics of a congregation moved to terror or joy by an evangelist. For them, the public, emotional outburst of the revival churches was "enthusiasm" and constituted "plain evidence of the weakness of human nature." Noisy emotionalism in the course of church services was the most dramatic dimension of revival. One critic described an Andrew Crosswell revival as follows:

The assembly came together about 11 o Clock before noon, some singing hymns as they came thro' the Streets (as was also done at other times) & being in the meeting house such was the noise thro' distress & joy, real or pretended, that the Ministers neither preached nor prayed, but Mr. Croswell went about the Meeting house Crying mercy, mercy, mercy sufficient in the blood of Christ for the chief of Sinners &c. and in such a frame they continued till 9 at night.

Jonathan Edwards defended such outbursts, as not necessarily of converting force but not contrary to it either. Here was a principal distinction between many moderates and the opposition. The moderates insisted that the essence of the Awakening did not reside in its excesses while opponents were equally certain that it did.

Although the revival's critics in any denomination and any region could agree on the excesses and evils they opposed while sharing a conviction that such excesses were not only characteristic but essential to the phenomenon, they did not always become opponents for the same reasons. Indeed, although it is fairly simple to outline the critique of the revival, describing its critics is much more difficult. Nevertheless, three distinct forms of opposition can be identified. One of these asserted that religion is a reasonable, orderly matter and not the passionate diversion it seemed to be in the hands of the revivalists. Such men were latitudinarians, religious "liberals," or, in the cant of the day, doctrinal "Arminians." Another body of opposition insisted that the existing social and ecclesiastical order—although imperfect—were essentially sound and ought not to be disturbed. Many such conservatives were also latitudinarians, but the religious life of the colonies was complex, and not all men sought to conserve liberal religion. One could both desire preservation of the social fabric and oppose revival without the slightest taint of broadmindedness. A third form of opposition, most common among the Quakers and a few other smaller sects, had so insulated their religion from the society in which they lived that they refused to become involved in the spiritual affairs of the wider world, even when these affairs included a revival they might otherwise approve. For such people, the Awakening was as much irrelevant as erroneous.

Perhaps the most striking feature of the opposition was its frequent insistence that the Awakening's supporters were enemies of "right reason." Benjamin Doolittle, a Yale graduate in the 1720s, complained in 1743 that the revivalists despised reason as an "evil and dangerous guide in matters of religion." Charles Chauncy was more positive, insisting "there is such a thing as real religion, and let the conduct of men be what it will; and 'tis in its nature a sober, calm reasonable thing." Such phrases characterized not only the statements of many Congregational and Presbyterian opponents but most of the Church of England clergy as well. Commissary Alexander Garden of South Carolina felt nothing but pity for those who responded to George Whitefield in 1741: "Alas, my poor fellow Creatures! Wilfully abandoning their *Reason,* (the alone distinguishing Dignity of their Nature!) Fleeing from it as from a Serpent. And throwing themselves into the Arms of strong Delusion." John Checkley of Philadelphia exalted in his "Arminianism," which he held "represents our holy Religion as a *reasonable* Service, the Glory and Ornament of our rational Nature and an Introduction to future Felicity."

The differences over the meaning of "right reason" between evangelicals and their opponents took a much more complicated form than a simple confrontation between rationality and irrationality. It is true that many New Lights (particularly in the radical wing) paid little attention to philosophical niceties and exalted immediate emotional impulses as direct gifts of God. It is equally true that for many opponents "reason" meant nothing more than common sense, which told them that one must be "reasonable" to avoid rocking the boat. But lurking in the background was a fundamental disagreement over the nature of human psychology. This disagreement was not between modernist opponents who believed in a rational universe and traditionalist revivalists who were committed to older ideas. In the context of the times, those who emphasized emotion were the innovators in terms of epistemology, the study of how man knows and thinks. The clash of psychological interpretation was most apparent in the famous debate between Charles Chauncy and Jonathan Edwards.

For Chauncy, religion's proof and strength were derived from the the orderly, comfortable, confident, and optimistic world of Newton. In part, Chauncy represented a branch of Puritan thought whose dedication to reason accompanied a new, low-key reassurance that man's chance for salvation was part of his capacity for self-improvement. His major work appeared as a direct refutation of Jonathan Edwards' *Some Thoughts Concerning the Present Revival of Religion in New England*. Titling his work *Seasonable Thoughts on the State of Religion in New England*—in obvious reference to Edwards' title—Chauncy offered an exhaustive, scholarly refutation of the Northampton minister's argument. Chauncy accepted a psychology which placed the mind and the emotions in separate categories. Thus he appealed to reason, which controlled emotion and directed the will; but each had its distinct compartment. This position had been dominant in Christian thought since the Middle Ages, and meant that Chauncy was a psychological traditionalist. For the Boston pastor, "there is the Religion of the Understanding and Judgment, and Will, as well as of the Affections; and if little account is made of the former, while great Stress is laid upon the latter . . . People should run into disorder."

Like most of those who emphasized rationalism, Chauncy not only separated reason and affection but insisted, in true medieval fashion, that the former must dominate the latter. The Anglican leader Samuel Johnson agreed wholeheartedly. Man's understanding, "which ought to be uppermost and preside," was, in the hands of the revivalists, "obliged basely to truckle to the inferior lusts and appetites." Moreover, said Johnson, the passions, "which ought to be governed by reason, and to be consistent and at unity one with another, are in a state of rebellion against the reason, and in a confused inconsistency and jumble and in a perpetual war one with another." However modern men like Chauncy and Johnson may have been in some intellectual areas, in their view of human nature they were unreconstructed traditionalists.

The commitment to compartmentalized psychological categories and to conflict between mind and emotion (to be won by the mind) was strongly denied by Jonathan Edwards. Perhaps too much can be made of Edwards' use of Lockean psychology in this regard, because most New Lights were not disciples of John Locke and were not interested in the intellectual complexities so lovingly considered by Edwards, but most revivalists concurred in the basic thrust of his argument. Edwards objected strenuously not only to a separation of the affections and the will (by which most contemporaries understood emotions and mind) but to a philosophy which identified the "affections of the soul" not with "the noblest part of the soul, but the meanest principles that it has, that belong to man, as partaking of animal nature, and what he has in common with the brute creation, rather than any thing whereby he is conformed to angels and pure spirits." He chose to counter such a demeaning view by uniting affections and will, and by insisting that "all acts of the will are truly acts of the affections." This was a truly modern position.

In *Some Thoughts* and the subsequent *Treatise Concerning Religious Affections* Edwards strove desperately to distinguish affections agreeable to truth and to error, in an attempt to separate his position from that of the radicals. Such careful distinctions were less understood, however, than Edwards' general thesis that "true religion lies very much in the affections." It was in terms of this thesis that Edwards was the spokesman of revival, for it was the heart of the difference between New Lights and Old Lights. Opponents of the revival always insisted that true religion must be in the understanding, which must triumph over lower animal passions. "I am not against the Preaching of Terror," wrote Charles Chauncy, "but whenever it is done, it ought to be done in a way that may enlighten the Mind as well as alarm the Passions."

The differing psychological perceptions of human nature had enormous ramifications in all areas of doctrine and church practice. If religion is reasonable and men are rational creatures, then surely man must play a conscious part in his own salvation, perhaps even willing it himself. Again, if religion is reasonable and men are rational, then all men should be admitted to the sacraments of the church. Thinking such as this, carried to its logical conclusion, had led more than one Puritan minister to the Church of England. For Anglicans, the Great Awakening was less a traumatic than an unfortunate experience. But to many individuals, clergy and layman alike, who had remained within traditional

Calvinist denominations, the revival was a frightening business. Many opponents saw in the Awakening dramatic illustrations of the dangers of emotionalism run rampant—the evils of "thinking" with the heart instead of the head. Outside the Church of England, the revival responded to an implicit Arminianism and produced opponents who were forced to be explicit about their beliefs. For New England Puritanism and Middle Colony Presbyterianism, pietism and Arminianism could no longer coexist within the same system.

Many men had used the reasonable approach to religion as the basis for accommodation to social conditions as they found them. This was particularly true of Anglicanism in the Southern colonies, where the dominant social ideal was that of the planters. Commissary Alexander Garden was simply incapable of comprehending George Whitefield's opposition to "balls and assemblies." To be against such social events was as unthinkable to Garden as to inveigh "against Friends, Neighbours, or Acquaintance meeting together to pass a Winter's Evening in their own private Houses." A similar acceptance of the values of urban mercantile society characterized many Northern clergymen. To tell a man who, through his own efforts, had been successful in commerce that such an approach would not work in religion was as unthinkable as opposing the planters' social values.

But not all opponents of the Awakening had synthesized latitudinarianism and social accommodation—which many had fought with the strength of their own authority, insisting on the maintenance of the "good old ways." Revivalists sought to return to the proper values, but were prepared to overturn traditional clerical authority through itinerancy and exaltation of the layman in order to achieve their ends. Many ministers had become too accustomed to "preaching down" to congregations (made up of both those who feared failure in the search for salvation and those who did not care) to be able to accept parishioners who felt they had sought and found a place among the saved. Itinerancy served as a symbol of social evil in the movement, for it meant social and institutional disruption of traditional patterns of clerical authority in inescapable terms.

Conservatives like Thomas Clap, President of Yale, had —before 1740—seen the dangers to clerical authority inherent in latitudinarian accommodation. They had opposed "Arminianism" with all their might. After 1740, such men used their powerful posts in the community to slow the revival's march toward social change. Most "Old Side" Presbyterian and Reformed clergy shared Clap's concern. Some opponents of revival had seen the dangers of itinerant preaching even before the coming of Whitefield. As early as 1731, Nathaniel Stone of Cape Cod responded to a lay preacher in his community with the comment:

> It tends to absolute confusion in all our instituted chhs; for, if he may take one part of my Flock to preach to; another may as well take another, and another a third; and what then becomes the Pastorall office into which, the Ministers are in a publick and solemn manner brought? Yea where is any flock for them to lead, if others may act according to this mans disorderly and aspiring humour, and practice!

Where, indeed, would any minister find a flock to *lead*? The choice of verbs was not accidental.

Both the accommodationalist and the authoritarian conservative tended, understandably, to equate ecclesiastical disruption with social leveling. "Some of the meanest and worst, of the People, are lately become converts to these Principles [of revivalism]," wrote Anglican missionary Isaac Browne in 1741, "and are sent about the country to preach to all that come in their way, and they make it their business to reproach the Clergy among the common people, to the great hinderance and discouragement of Religion in these Parts." The itinerants, according to Browne, included "a poor illiterate Weaver, another a Carpenter, a third an ignorant Schoolmaster, and a little before those about 4 or 5 common Ploughmen undertook to teach and expound upon Sundays."

Most opponents of the revival shared Browne's concern for the unleashing of lay exhorters, and in many cases may have exaggerated the "commonness" of the itinerants. But the opposition understood full well the relationship between ecclesiastical and social order, and felt that both had to be maintained simultaneously. Moderate New Lights had begun the revival in the belief that ecclesiastical order could be maintained, and even restored, by disturbing the fabric of society. As it became increasingly clear to moderates that the opponents of the revival were correct in their criticisms, most moderates defended ecclesiastical order at any cost, which left only the radicals as the main supporters of unfettered revivalism.

For some colonial Americans, the Awakening was less opposed than ignored. Such a response was particularly characteristic of members of the Society of Friends. The Quakers, who in the seventeenth century had operated with values and practices which had a good deal in common with the revival, had by 1740 retreated too far from colonial society in their religious practices to permit themselves to be affected by these latest social outbursts. Persecution outside Pennsylvania and the incompatibility of Quaker ideals with expansionist secular values within that province combined to force the Friends within themselves. The absence of a distinct clergy, which might have responded to the Awakening, undoubtedly contributed to the Quakers' insularity. There was no clerical leadership to force the Friends to confront the revival, and so, as John Greenleaf Whittier later put it,

The Quaker kept the way of his own, —
A non-conductor among the wires,
with coat of asbestos proof to fires.

The occasional small sect, which survived in the larger society by withdrawal, responded as did the Quakers. The Baptists of New England, for example, succeeded in remaining almost completely aloof from the Awakening proper. They were forced to come to terms with revival only in the 1760s, when they were overwhelmed by a new wave of Baptists from the Awakening's radical wing.

Those religious groups which remained immune to revivalism neither gained nor lost by their stance. For those opponents who took position on the issues of the Awakening, however, there were both immediate practical advantages and considerable long-range liabilities. In the short run, those denominations (such as the Anglicans) and those clergy who were known for their opposition to the revival experienced considerable gains among laymen who shared their antagonism. A number of Old Light churches were formed in areas dominated by evangelical clergymen, and the Anglicans expanded in both New England and the Middle Colonies. John Miln of New Jersey spoke for many of his Church of England colleagues when, in 1744, he commented that

> After the Ravages of Enthusiasm which like a Epidemical distemper raged all over America but chiefly here, the Church is again restored to a much better state, the Congregations being now frequented by men of the best sense who formerly were of other sects, or supinely negligent about Religion but have been by this stirred up to enquire, having been in general deceived in their expectation by large impudent pretence to supernatural gifts, but finding no proof but grimace.

Over time, however, the opposition discovered that setting its face resolutely against revivalism cut it off from a substantial number of Americans, especially those in the back country. In the South, the Church of England lost much of its dominance because of its inability to serve the moving frontier, and "reasonable" religion found itself confined largely to the settled areas of the Eastern seacoast.

In the end, few Americans could remain unaffected by the revival. For five years of religious ferment, colonial intellectual leaders had debated what for them were the critical issues of the day. The colonial mind of 1745, when the debate had lost its edge, was far different than it had been in 1740. Attitudes toward the use of reason and the meaning of social order had been profoundly complicated. No one could approach such doctrinal matters as free will, election, assurance, or the religious affections—or more general philosophical questions dealing with epistemology—in innocence of their consequences within the context of a great mass movement. The Awakening had sharpened so many things by virtue of its sheer quantity. Many found their thinking profoundly shaped by the experiences of revival; all found their ideas had been influenced by the Great Awakening.

CHAPTER SEVEN

Impact of the Awakening: Numbers and Demographic Characteristics

The Day of the Power of Christ comes at once upon us, and they are almost together, both Whites and Blacks, both Old and Young, both Prophane and Moral, awakened, and made alive to God.

—Thomas Prince to George Whitefield, December 6, 1741

Much of our information about the number of individuals converted and their characteristics derives from accounts of contemporaries of the Great Awakening. Such accounts were usually produced either for didactic or polemical purposes. Supporters of the revival, naturally enough, chose to emphasize the comprehensiveness of the Awakening's appeal both numerically and socially. They wanted the revival to be understood as "great and general." Such a perception was essential to their defense of the movement as a work of God. Opponents of the revival, on the other hand, tended to deprecate the numbers permanently affected, insisting that the Awakening's appeal was principally to minorities which did not really matter. The subjects of revival were "Women, Children, Servants, and Nigros," as one observer put it. Some areas of disagreement between the two hostile impressions are not impossible to reconcile, but most contemporary accounts of the revival have affected subsequent histories while providing little basis upon which to effect a reconciliation of the conflicting testimonies.

Both pro- and anti-revival assessments of the Awakening's popularity were obviously influenced by what the observers wanted to believe. The New Light insistence upon the general nature of the revival has been particularly detrimental to any efforts to understand the underlying nonreligious implications in terms of both cause and effect. If the revival cut a general swath across the geographical, social, and economic characteristics of the society at large, then none of these factors can be vitally explanatory. Not surprisingly, those who have accepted the "great and general" view of the appeal of the Awakening have fallen back not simply on nonsecular explanations of the phenomenon but frequently on otherworldly ones. In such explanations, historians have echoed the New Lights, who saw the Awakening as divinely inspired. Thus the question of popular appeal must be dealt with apart from either New Light or Old Light assumptions.

Numbers

In the absence of any hard data, those who record the number of "converts" produced by the Great Awakening have been limited only by their attitude toward revivalism and by the total population of the American colonies in 1740 (something just under one million, many of whom were small children). Thus estimates have varied from a low "few thousand" to as high as "half a million." The latter is obviously suspect, given the population figures.

The problems involved in obtaining precise data for revivals are many, and the relevant records for the colonial period are lacking in most areas, particularly in the Middle Colonies and the South. But even if such records were available, there would still be problems of definition. Modern revivalists keep precise records, but still they cannot satisfy the critics. Many who have suddenly been converted in revival meetings may have equally suddenly backslid, a point the opponents of the Awakening always made. Should "one day" converts be counted? Others, though genuinely converted, may, for one reason or another, have taken no action to leave any record of their experiences. They may not even have formally joined a church. And, of course, not everyone agreed or agrees on what constitutes genuine conversion.

Given the difficulty of definition, the act of becoming a formal church member is virtually the only yardstick for measuring numbers. Joining a church meant leaving some kind of record of one's religious commitment. Moreover, many contemporaries did not consider an individual converted if he did not join a church. For many ministers, the whole point of revival was to increase church membership, and for most, the act of conversion was not completed until the individual had been "brought sensibly to Christ" and joined one of Christ's visible churches.

Although surviving church records are, at best, scattered and incomplete, and virtually nonexistent outside New England, some notion of the popular impact of revival, as measured in terms of church membership, can be gained from data gathered for two regions of New England: Connecticut and southeastern Massachusetts. The relative similarity of the figures from the two regions suggests that the data, when averaged, may fairly closely approximate the number of admissions for New England as a whole in the period covered by the data. The extrapolation from these two regions to New England is defensible on several grounds: the regions are substantial ones, the data are similar, and there is no evidence in any of the contemporary literary sources to suggest that experiences in these regions were considered particularly unusual (see Table I).

Table I. Average Number of Annual Admissions to Particular Churches in Two Regions of New England, per Church, 1733-1747.

Year	Southeastern Massachusetts*	Connecticut†
1733	6.3	8.5
1734	5.7	7.5
1735	4.4	19.5
1736	14.1	12.5
1737	7.0	8.7
1738	5.6	11.2
1739	4.8	8.5
1740	4.9	7.3
1741	8.0	43.4
1742	37.4	22.7
1743	12.3	5.2
1744	4.9	4.5
1745	3.5	3.8
1746	2.3	3.3
1747	2.0	3.5

*Figures based on table in J. M. Bumsted, "The Pilgrim's Progress: The Ecclesiastical History of Southeastern Massachusetts," unpublished Ph.D. dissertation, Brown University (1965), pp. 290-291.

†Figures based on table in H. F. Vos, "The Great Awakening in Connecticut," unpublished Ph.D. dissertation, Northwestern University (1967), pp. 171-172.

Connecticut's slightly higher annual figures probably reflect a larger population served by a particular church. Per capita, there were fewer churches in Connecticut than in southeastern Massachusetts. The increased admissions in the mid-1730s, particularly in Connecticut, represent the Edwards revivals, which hit geographically contiguous Connecticut (especially the Connecticut River Valley) harder than more distant southeastern Massachusetts. Chronologically and in terms of numbers, southeastern Massachusetts also lagged behind Connecticut in the early 1740s—again, probably because of communications. But taking an average of the churches in the two regions for the period 1741–1744 gives the following mean annual admissions per church:

1741	25.7
1742	30.0
1743	8.8
1744	4.7

The four-year total of 69.2, multiplied by the approximately 400 churches in New England during the period, yields a total for admissions to church membership during the revival years of around 27,000. This is a substantial figure, and would seem to bear out contemporary claims of "Thousands Converted." Nevertheless, this total (which, if anything, is generous in terms of the number of admissions) must be further examined, in the light of admission figures for periods before and after 1741–1744 and in terms of other significant characteristics of those who joined churches in the revival years.

One interesting and important result of recent and careful investigation of individual, local revivals in particular churches in New England is the discovery that those who joined churches during the revival were, on the average, six years younger than those who had joined before 1740. Such a finding substantiates claims made at the time by many New Light pastors (and by a number of hostile Old Light critics as well) that the Awakening had a special appeal to the young in their parishes. From the standpoint of attempting to ascertain the numbers converted during the revival, the chief value of these data is to help explain the very low number of admissions in the years immediately following the Awakening. Over the long run, the low number of admissions after 1743 is crucial.

Looking again at the figures in Table I, we see that the admission totals for the seven years preceding 1740 can be compared with the totals for the next seven years (Table II).

Table II. Average Number of Admissions to Particular Churches in Two Regions of New England, 1733-1739 and 1740-1746

Years	Southeastern Massachusetts	Connecticut	Average
1733–39	47.9	75.4	61.7
1740–46	73.3	90.2	81.8

One of the obvious weaknesses of contemporary claims for the number who were converted in the revival is that people were *always* being converted, *always* joining churches. Thus the issue should not be "gross" conversions but the net gains of the Awakening years over ordinary times.

Table II enables us to compute some net gains, which turn out to be an average of twenty per church. When multiplied by the total number of New England churches (approximately 400), the total *net gain* is just over 8,000. Since low admissions prevail for nearly twenty years after 1743, comparison of admissions for twenty years before the Awakening and for twenty years after it would virtually eliminate any net gain. If the revival had a net gain of 8,000 church members in New England (to which must be added perhaps several thousand who joined churches outside the establishment or had no churches to join), this represents a substantial proportion of the population over sixteen. But the Great Awakening did not greatly increase the number of church members in New England *over the long run*. It appears, instead, to have drawn on a fairly constant pool of individuals who would eventually have joined churches anyway. Colonial Americans accepted religion as a central feature of their lives, and the revival appealed to a population willing—even anxious—to join churches. Not totals, but timing, is the important factor.

The real numerical significance of the revival is that it got more individuals into the churches at once and at an earlier age than had previously been typical. Moreover, it supplied church members who shared a common experience and who brought similar religious values and assumptions into the churches. Finally, because the revival appealed to a somewhat different segment of the population than had previously joined churches (besides simply being younger), the demographic profile of membership in particular churches was suddenly and drastically altered. All this is crucial for understanding the significance of the Awakening. But in New England, and by extension probably in other settled regions of America, the impact of revival cannot really be measured in terms of numbers converted.

In defense of the revival's numerical effect, it must be noted that the above analysis does not deal with individuals in frontier regions who had no established churches to join. The lack of records for ephemeral churches on the moving frontier makes it impossible to calculate the numbers converted in the back country, where perhaps numbers were the significant point. But in settled regions of America, over the long run they were not.

Demographic Characteristics

Although the Awakening may not have appreciably affected church membership numerically, it had considerable impact on membership in other ways. In the first place, the new converts were substantially younger than had been the case before 1740. Secondly, long-standing patterns of the sex ratio were temporarily altered among those admitted to membership; for a brief time, more males than females entered the churches. Finally, the two most important racial minorities in colonial America—the blacks and the Indians—figured much more prominently in the white man's religious activities during the revival years than they had previously. Detailed evidence for these points, as for the number converted, is available only for New England, but there is no reason to assume that the situation elsewhere in America was any different. Certainly the contemporary literary evidence does not suggest regional variation.

Accounts of local revivals, published in *Christian History* and elsewhere, rang the recurrent theme of the relative youth of the new converts. From Wrentham, Massachusetts, came an account of "almost daily . . . new instances of young persons (for the work of God's Spirit seemed to be chiefly on young people) in great concern, what they should do to be saved." In Newark, New Jersey, the change was mainly in "the rising generation," and visible for the most part among "the younger people."

Recent detailed analyses of admissions in individual churches in New England substantiate the literary evidence and indicate the dimensions of the shift. In Norton, Massachusetts, for example, the average age of those admitted to communion before 1740 had been 39.7 years, and only 21.6 percent of these were under age thirty. During the revival, the average age of male admissions was 29.9: 71.3 percent were under thirty and 57 percent were between twenty and thirty. The average age of admissions in Middleborough, Massachusetts—which had a substantial number of converts—dropped from thirty-five to twenty-seven, and more than two-thirds (72.6 percent) were under the age of thirty. Similar figures have been worked out for Andover, Massachusetts. During the revival the admission ages probably approximated the age profiles of the general colonial population more closely than in the pre-1740 statistics, but the shift was nevertheless marked and different. The young were significantly affected by the Awakening.

What did this shift in the age pattern of church membership mean? It appears to have altered the community significance of membership in the church. Where previously the churches had been the domain of the older and more established members of the community, they were now open to all. Moreover, this change may have indicated a shift in the accepted age of full adulthood and community responsibility, although it is not clear whether the revival served in this respect as cause or effect. But if church membership was a mark of adult responsibility, younger residents of the community were gaining this status.

As was true of the younger age of conversion, the alteration in the sex ratio also was frequently remarked upon by contemporaries. Even before 1740, Jonathan Edwards had noted a difference in his Northampton revival—as he wrote in his *Faithful Narrative*:

> I hope that more than 300 souls were savingly brought home to Christ, in this town, in the space of half a year, and about the same number of males as females. By what I have heard Mr. Stoddard say, this was far from what has been usual in years past; for he observed that in his time, many more women were converted than men.

Peter Thacher of Middleborough also observed, in 1744, that "in the ordinary Excitations of Grace before this Time, there were more *Females* added than *Males*, as I suppose has been usual in other churches; but in this extraordinary season, the Grace of God has surprisingly seized and subdued the hardiest men, and more Males have been added here than the tenderer sex."

Again, detailed study in substantiating the literary evidence has been carried out only for New England, but the results for some representative "awakened" churches are revealing. The data indicate how common the shift in sex ratio was, and suggest that it probably occurred everywhere in America (see Table III). The increases in male membership were gratifying to ministers for several reasons. Not only did they mean that the entire community was affected, but these additional males, committed to the ideals of the church, strengthened the church's political position in the community in an age when only males were enfranchised. Such a shift in the sex ratio and the appeal to the male population substantiate the notion that somehow the Awakening was involved in a redefinition of the meaning of adulthood.

The important point about the effect of the revival on minority groups is not that they were "getting religion," for all denominations had long maintained a missionary commitment to the Indians and admitted a duty to Christianize blacks (although more often rhetorically than actually). Instead of being objects of missionary efforts, which might have resulted in the formation of distinct minority churches, both the Indians and the blacks, during the height of the Awakening, became part of the general movement. They attended revival meetings and were incorporated into previously all-white churches.

Much of the best evidence of the integrative tendencies of the Awakening comes from unsympathetic accounts of revivals by those who were hostile to the phenomenon. Social conservatives recognized the innovation, and were appalled by it. In Plymouth, Massachusetts, for example, Josiah Cotton complained of the New Lights that there "was the utmost confusion in their meetings, some Singing, some crying some laughing for Joy, others opposing &c., all at once, & the Pulpit filt with Boys & a Negro or two who were directed to invite others to come to Christ." A particularly revealing account of a New Light meeting was printed in 1745 in the *Boston Evening Post:*

> And now if you have any Tincture of Enthusiasm, cry, laugh, rowl your Eyes, and work up your Imagination, to see what has never been seen since the triumphant March of Dr. Sacheverell's Mob. The Meeting-House being denied them, the Stage must be erected near it, and you well know who are the Persons that generally mount Stages. Here you might see a strapping Fellow take up a great Crutch and stagger away under the Weight of it. There you might see others dragging and sweating with their long Poles. Some marched in solemn Procession with their Instruments to fix the Poles and the Crutches. But what moved my pity most, was a poor old Negro Man that could hardly support the Infirmities of his Age, hawling and puffing at a large Crowbar, and had I not known the Occasion of the Show, I should have concluded he was the subject of their Assembling: But the poor Creature had Compassion shown him, and was relieved by a zealous Brother, who stuck the Bar in the Ground, standing over it with his under Lip hanging down . . . as if the whole Burden of Church and State was laid upon his under Jaw. . . . Alas, what will not Enthusiasm do?

Enthusiasm was obviously a major factor in breaking down color bars, at least temporarily. It also quickened the tempo of missionary activities among minority groups. George Whitefield, it is true, supported slavery and employed slaves on his Georgia lands, but he also reemphasized the importance of Christianizing the Negro. Everywhere in colonial America a new generation of missionaries to the Indians appeared, including such noteworthies as Eleazer Wheelock, James Davenport, David Brainerd, and (for a time) Jonathan Edwards. Wheelock's activities produced the first Indian evangelist in Samson Occum and the first institution of higher learning for Indians in North America, later Dartmouth College.

Brainerd had particular success in bringing the revival to the Indians, although those who were already somewhat acculturated responded best. At Crosswicks, near Freehold, New Jersey, where there had been a revival among the white population a number of years earlier, his missionary efforts brought exciting results: "It was remarkable that, as fast as they [Indians] came from remote places round about, the Spirit of God seemed to seize them with concern for their souls."

In the Southern colonies, where the bulk of Negroes was located, the Awakening's impact is more difficult to measure. The only evidence for the meaning of the revival to the Southern slave comes from missionaries and planters, particularly the former. The white inhabitants of the South had long had mixed feelings toward the slave and Christianity; and the Anglican church mounted sporadic campaigns at Christianizing the Negroes through baptism and religious education. Whatever the church's intentions, such efforts were always justified to planter society in terms of social control. One Virginia minister explained to the Bishop of London in 1722: "I have prevailed with some of my parishioners to suffer their slaves to be instructed in the christian religion & baptized, for which they have since thank'd me, having found them both more trusty & more diligent in their service than they were before." But many planters fiercely opposed such action, "being led away by the notion of their being and becoming worse slaves when Christians." The underlying concern, wrote Commissary James Blair in 1729, was that most Negroes accepted Christianity "only . . . in hopes that they shall meet with so much the more respect, and that some time or other Christianity will help them to their freedom."

The planters found grounds for their concern in 1730, when a Virginia slave uprising was feared, involving Negroes "angry and saucy" because baptism had failed to free them. Many slaveholders argued that baptism into the Christian church made the Negroes "prouder, and inspires them with thoughts of freedom." If Negro membership in the Anglican communion before 1740 was regarded as dangerous by many Southerners, conversion to one of the evangelical churches after 1740 was potentially more dangerous. White evangelicals in the South emphasized that planters' fears were unjustified by preaching Negro quietism even more desperately than the Anglicans, and they insisted that any implications of equality before God did not apply on earth but only in heaven. Religious conversion may have encouraged many planters to permit their slaves to be admitted to Christianity, but the evangelical churches in the South were even firmer on the obligations of slaves than was the Anglican church.

Eventually, however, the impulses of revivalism had their effect on Negro society in the South. Small evangelical churches, founded by black preachers, began to spring up in Southern cities after the American Revolution. While Northern Negroes may have achieved an increased sense of dignity and identity through membership in white churches, only the black churches in the South could employ religion to enhance the position of their members. The Negro churches appealed to freed blacks and to highly skilled slaves, most of whom were confined to the urban centers. Their status was more a product of the new philosophies let loose by the Revolution and by changing economic conditions in the South than a direct result of the Great Awakening. But the black evangelists had absorbed both the techniques and the doctrinal assumptions of the revival.

Demography and Revolution

In terms of modern analyses of movements of social protest and revolution, the particular demographic appeal of the Great Awakening suggests that a proto-revolutionary force was inherent in revivalism. The Awakening appealed to the young and to oppressed minorities, which traditionally are the breeding ground for new notions of social, political, and economic change. Nevertheless, neither the temporarily altered patterns of church membership nor the events of the 1740s produced major upheavals in colonial American society. Indeed, the Great Awakening may have helped to prevent great social upheavals instead of fostering them.

This possibility should surprise no one who has lived in North America through the 1960s. The fact that the revival did not lead to an altered society should not, however, immediately label it as reactionary or counterrevolutionary. We have seen in our own times the emergence of alternative styles for dealing with an unacceptable social system. One style emphasizes the overthrow of the system by means of violent political action while another stresses withdrawal from corruption into a private world of drugs, rural communes, and exotic personal beliefs. Those who have been involved understand very well the differences between the super-rational dialecticalism of revolutionary radicalism and the irrational (even antirational) assumptions of the drop-out culture. They are also aware that the "establishment" is equally fearful of both styles, since both challenge traditional values in different ways. The system frequently finds it more difficult to cope with irrationalism it does not comprehend than with revolutionaries it can politically repress.

Given the nature of the tensions and problems which faced Americans in 1740, an observer might well have diagnosed a society on the verge of upheaval. Certain members of that society, particularly the young, had obvious reasons for discontent. Instead of a political or social revolution, however, what colonial America experienced in the 1740s was a spiritual reawakening based upon an appeal to human needs other than right reason. This revival caught up the potentially disruptive. The result was an emphasis upon individual inward change rather than upon externally directed reform or revolution. The speed and intensity of the changes and their effect upon Americans and their institutions during the Great Awakening had an obvious revolutionary potential, and occasionally produced it. But the process of conversion combined with the new attitudes and values of the converts to militate against secular revolution. Had the "awakened" chosen to overthrow government, they might well have succeeded; their descendants certainly did. But revolution was not seen as an option by either the leadership or those converted in the Awakening, at least not in a political sense. There was only one movement of protest to join, and the nature of pietism tended to restrict one's view to the individual soul and its relationship with God, channeling any fervor for change largely into ecclesiastical concerns.

The accepted view of the social impact of the Great Awakening has been best stated by Edwin S. Gaustad, who emphasized that the "religious turmoil" of New England "was in fact 'great and general' in that it knew no boundaries, social or geographical, that it was both urban and rural, and that it reached both lower and upper classes." Such a generalization eliminates and dismisses social conflict instead of recognizing the possibility that the revival was spawned out of conflicts that it resolved. That the Awakening touched almost everyone is indisputable, but it nevertheless had special appeal for certain segments of the population. Accepting this fact permits one to understand some of the factors which led Americans in the 1740s to ask "What must I do to be saved?" And the revival's opponents can be recognized as more than simply factious in their criticisms. The Great Awakening was a movement which appealed to potentially explosive social and political elements, a point that was sensed by an opposition concerned for its own central place in the society as then constituted.

The revival, then, was a movement of rebellion rather than revolution. Its internal logic tended to defuse overt attacks on society. Obvious illustrations of the effect of revivalism in rechanneling secular discontents can be found in some of the later frontier extensions of the Great Awakening. In the Carolinas in the early 1770s, for example, back-country revolts against Eastern domination (the so-called Regulator movements) slowly fizzled out under the eruption of evangelical religion. The simultaneous presence of discontent and pietism indicates the shared roots of revolution and revival. Similarly, in Nova Scotia at the time of the American Revolution, a Yankee population which ought to have supported its New England relations in rebellion against the Crown instead quite deliberately chose to withdraw from politics and support a movement of religious pietism. Henry Alline, the evangelist who was most responsible for the revival in Nova Scotia, stressed the unimportance of the "earthly city" and the need for personal salvation.

But the Awakening's record was not entirely negative in social terms. As we shall see in the next chapter, although pietism tended to turn men's attention from the injustice of this world, it could also, under certain conditions, provide a faith which made fighting possible. Moreover, the force of the movement frequently created effects not deliberately intended by anyone. In many respects, the revival produced results as perplexing and paradoxical as the inception and course of the movement. Just as no single factor explains the Great Awakening, no single adjective can define it.

CHAPTER EIGHT

Impact of the Awakening: Social and Political Characteristics

We whose Names are hereunto Subsribed humbly Sheweth that GOD has [given] to every Man an Unalianable Right in Matters of His Worship to [act] for himself as his Consciance reseves the Rule from GOD & hath Blessed [those] that hath appeared to stand uprightly for the Liberty of Consciance in all Ages.
–Petition of the Separates of Massachusetts to the General Court, June 7, 1749

The Great Awakening was a complex movement, which is difficult to generalize about. Nowhere is this more obvious than in terms of its impact upon colonial society. Every general statement can be matched not only with an exception but by an almost diametrically opposite general statement. Such paradoxical results should not be surprising from a movement which abounded in paradoxes: its general thrust was toward egalitarianism among the saints while it self-righteously read the unconverted out of human existence; a preoccupation with guilt and sin while striving for their extirpation; an emphasis upon human commitment and reform while denying the individual's ability to achieve them by himself; and an insistence upon the rights of the converted in this world while refusing to acknowledge worldly authority.

Many of the converted tended to side with one extreme or the other. Moreover, what the revival's proponents tended to view as blessings were the same developments which opponents saw as evils and excesses. Contemporary opinion itself seemed paradoxical. Finally, the different conditions and circumstances in the many locales of America affected by revival make generalization difficult. What seemed to be change for the better in one area could be less functional in others. Assessing the impact of the Awakening in terms of standards of conduct, social reform among the races, community integration, and political meaning will, therefore, always be difficult and subject to controversy.

Standards of Conduct

What they perceived as an appalling state of morality in their parishes continually distressed the American clergy—of this much we can be certain. Some of the concern, particularly in New England, was part of the long tradition of the jeremiad, which attempted to explain the decline of the "City on a Hill" by attributing increasingly sinful behavior to its inhabitants, which displeased God. As early as the 1670s, one could find catalogues of moral degeneracy which stressed increased drunkenness, "backbiting," fornication, and—the worst offense of all—lack of commitment to the churches and their goals. Some of the clerical anguish over fallen congregations is attributable to the Calvinistic belief in weak and evil men (original sin), but there seems to be no reason to dismiss the complaints of the ministers out of hand. Whether or not immorality was increasing relative to an earlier generation of more committed settlers is immaterial. Colonials *did* drink heavily, perhaps to assuage their anxieties, and there were many taverns; deviation from the sexual standards of the time *was* common; and not everyone accepted the strict moral standards of the Christian churches.

If a high level of immorality was one of the classic complaints of the clergy before the revival, the revival's effect upon moral conduct would inevitably become a test of its efficacy. Not surprisingly, most of the New Light testimony emphasized success in this area. As Nathaniel Leonard of Plymouth, Massachusetts, wrote:

> For some months together, you should scarcely see any body at the taverns, unless they were strangers, travellers, or some come there upon necessary business. The children forsook their plays in the streets, and persons of all denominations, except a few, gave themselves to reading the word of God, and other books of devotion, to meditation, prayer, conference, and other religious exercises, and refrained from their customary vices. And many that lived at a distance, being acquainted with this town in its former state, coming hither, beheld us now with admiration, saying, Surely the fear of God is in this place.

But in Plymouth, as elsewhere, the general reformation was only temporary, confined to the height of the religious excitement. The situation soon became as before, leaving ministers like Leonard only the possibility of rejoicing in the permanent reformation of those who had actually been converted. Nevertheless, short-term alterations were visible, and were seldom denied even by opponents of the Awakening.

However, not all observers of the course of the revival were prepared to rejoice in testimonies of improved morality by its supporters. The most typical reservation came from those who objected to the principle of enforced social conformity, to the tendency of the New Lights to assume that anyone who did not behave as they did was no true Christian. As one of Nathaniel

Leonard's opponents in Plymouth put it:

> The Consequences of these things were great additions to the
> Church & something of a reformation, or rather alteration, for it
> is a doubt with me whether a change from open profaneness &
> irreligion to enthusiasm & rash Judging of others be a proper
> Judgmation, calling others that did not run the same length, &
> were for more order & decency Pharisees & opposers of the
> work of God &c.

Only well after the revival had cooled did anyone seriously attack it for having promoted immorality. In 1747 Doctor William Douglass of Boston, the irascible opponent of Cotton Mather in the smallpox controversy of the '20s, charged that the Awakening had promoted "Wantonness between the Sexes" by encouraging converts of both sexes to embrace one another in emotional revival meetings.

Some enthusiastic proponents of revival pushed past acceptable limits of deviation. A few extremists carried their conversions to a logical conclusion which contemporaries described as "antinomianism," being so assured of their special election and direct communion with God that they were no longer bound by the laws of man. In some cases this led directly to deviant sexual behavior. Members of one group in southeastern Massachusetts in the 1750s, for example, argued that their purity permitted them to leave their spouses and live with spiritual soul mates. A girl in Attleborough, whose "spiritual" relationship with a man not her husband was such that "they lay with the Bible between them," became pregnant by her soul mate. Such extreme behavior was as vociferously condemned by most revivalists as by Old Lights, partly because it brought the movement into disrepute but mainly from genuine horror at the nature of the activities.

Concern about the mingling of the sexes in emotional revival meetings, which in the back country could go on for days, merged with an occasional example of deviancy to produce the most extreme contemporary criticisms of the Awakening as an instrument of immorality. Such criticism came in sermons by the Southern Anglican itinerant Charles Woodmason, who charged:

Nothing more leads to this (Lasciviousness, or Wantonness, Adultery or Fornication) Than what they call their Love Feasts and Kiss of Charity. . . . The Assignations made on Sundays at the Singing Clubs, are here realized. And it is no wonder that Things are as they are, when many Young Persons have 3.4.5.6 Miles to walk home in the Dark Night, with Convoy, thro' the Woods? Or staying perhaps all Night at some Cabbin (as on Sunday Nights) and sleeping together either doubly or promiscuously? Or a girl being mounted behind a Person to be carried home, or any wheres.

Obviously, a good deal depended on the perceptions of the critic, and on how sympathetic he was to the activities of the young.

Whatever went on at revival meetings, they produced an increased incidence of public confessions of wrongdoing, mainly sexual irregularities. Such confessions as the following (from Freetown, Massachusetts) were common:

I do now publickly acknowledge that I have fallen into the Sin of Fornication & thereby sinned against God in the Breach of the 7th Commandment for which I desire to take Shame and Confusion of Face to myself before God & Men particularly of the Chh of Christ in this Place.

Yet such evidence, however interesting and significant for our understanding of colonial sexual standards, scarcely provides any basis for assertions about the relationship of revivalism and morality beyond the obvious concern of the Awakening with sin.

The connection between sinfulness and conversion is complex. If we disregard the Old Light assertion that more confessions meant that the newly converted of the Awakening were more sinful, several suggestions can be advanced. One is that the confessions provide evidence of an increased sense of guilt about deviant behavior. In terms of the emphasis of most revival preachers, this would be entirely understandable. Part of the process of awakening was an increased awareness of sinfulness, and many people in the early stages of conversion would discover the evils of their activities and seek expiation through public confession (which in New England was a long-established habit). Such statements were good and proper form:

> I acknowledge my Self a Sinner both by nature & by Practice; that I was born into the World a Guilty object of Gods Wrath and a filthy Object of his Abhorrence: And that I went on Securely and Presumptuously Sinning against God notwithstanding many Solemn Warnings given me by the Word and Providence of God till about twelve Months past when God by his Wise & holy Providence awakened me in Some Measure.

Many converts undoubtedly made similar confessions.

But while some may have had their sense of guilt awakened, many others may have found revival a vehicle for the release of a longstanding and conscious concern about their behavior, such as the following:

> After Some Time thro Neglect of pubblick Worship and Bad Company I grew Careles again and fell in to Sin, especially that Sin for which I stand ready to make pubblick Confession when Cal'd to it. And now I began to flatter my Self that when I Come to be Settled in the World I shou'd have more time to mind the Business of Religion. But when I Come to Settle in a family I found my Cares greate and my Time les than before & this put me to Conclude it would never be better. Therefore I resolved to try to live a better Life then. But the more I tryed the worse I found my Self.

In this case, the Awakening only completed a process of personal understanding.

Whether the revival generated or exploited a feeling of guilt (one already eating away at the individual), it typically provided a therapeutic sense of release. All available accounts of conversion during the Awakening, whether by highly intellectualized clergymen or their parishioners, emphasize the exhilarating feeling of relief:

> As I was tending my Child I lift up my Heart to God, and I hade
> such a sense of the Love of God in Christ as overcome me and
> for a few moments I thote my Self in another World, & from this
> Time I felt ravished with the love of Christ . . .which thro Grace
> I obtained Comfortable Satisfaction that I was become a new
> Creature in Christ Jesus.

Such euphoria, experienced by those who had been saved for God,
was a distinguishing quality of the revival. Even if we can draw no
firm conclusions about the effect of the revival on morality, we can
note the Awakening's undoubted effect in relieving the burdensome anxieties of the individual sinner.

Aside from its undoubted effects on individual converts, only
two assertions can safely be made about the relationship of the
Great Awakening and public morality. During the height of local
revivals, a "public reformation" of the visible behavior of colonial
Americans *did* occur. For a short time at least, fewer people visited
taverns and more attended religious services. At least publicly, the
population exhibited patterns of behavior that were approved by
the standards of traditional Christian morality. What they did
behind closed doors is impossible to say, and opponents then and
since have been suspicious of the sincerity of the reformation.
Furthermore, the preaching of the Awakening revived familiarity
with traditional Christian virtues in America. It restated them in
most places and introduced them to others. This was particularly
critical in the back country, where the absence of organized religion had resulted in a decline of the values of traditional morality.

Social Injustice

The revival had little effect in altering basic patterns of social
inequity and injustice in America. As a spiritual movement, the
Awakening's natural concern was with the other world rather than
the existing, secular one in which the revival occurred. In the
pietist terms of reference, radicalism was typically measured by the
degree to which one *rejected* the affairs of this world. One of the
Awakening's greatest criticisms of the Arminians, latitudinarians,
and rationalists, who made up much of the opposition to revival,

was that these people were far too willing to accommodate themselves to the secular world. One needed to be radical to break with the intellectual conventions of the time, and radical New Lights tended to wrest themselves so completely from the world that they found it difficult to be concerned with the temporal woes of its disinherited. For them, oppression and injustice were spiritual rather than social or economic matters. Secular reform was more likely to grow out of the assumptions and preoccupations of the Old Lights rather than those of the New Lights.

The spiritual emphasis of the revival upon the individual and his soul made it difficult for evangelists to bother with the erection of secular institutions which might produce a force for change. The major institution of the Awakening was the church. With the exception of Whitefield's Bethesda orphanage and Eleazer Wheelock's Indian college in New Hampshire, the revival had remarkably little institutional effect on the society at large.

Not even the most ardent defenders of the Great Awakening as an instrument of change have been able to cite many illustrations of conscious secular reform. Indeed, modern critics of eighteenth-century revivalism—particularly in England—have seen it as a deflection of social improvement for the oppressed. Revivalism focused the attention of the disinherited upon salvation rather than upon organization and pressure upon the ruling and exploiting classes. For some critics, revivalism even became an instrument of the ruling interests for continued oppression of the lower orders. Such a critique echoes Marx's famous dictum that religion is "the opiate of the masses." An eighteenth-century revivalist would not easily have seen himself as a tool of the rulers, and even if he had, he would undoubtedly have rejected the notion. New Lights, particularly those whose origins were outside the ruling classes (such as the Separates and Separate Baptists), were convinced that opposition to revival was the conscious policy of those in power. For Separate leaders like Ebenezer Frothingham or Isaac Backus, the rulers were oppressive because their concerns were secular and because they opposed the ultimate reformation, which was personal spiritual regeneration. Eighteenth-century pietistic radicalism tended to reject all secular change as only ameliorative and palliative.

Only the radicals could hope to escape the conventions of the time—which for most moderate New Lights was impossible. Many moderates joined their Old Light opponents in various efforts at social improvement, usually through the churches; and the activities of Samuel Davies of Virginia were typical in this respect. Davies' parish was in Hanover County, the center of the plantation country, and his parishioners included many Negro slaves who sat in the meeting house "eagerly attentive to every word they hear, and frequently bathed in tears." Davies, who admitted Negroes to his church, by 1755 had baptized over 100 Negroes and claimed 300 as regular churchgoers. As part of his ministerial effort, he insisted upon education of the Negro. He concentrated on bringing books to the slaves, and his own account of his efforts indicates his assumptions:

> I am told, that in almost every house in my congregation and in sundry other places, they spend every leisure hour in trying to learn, since they expect *Books* as soon as they are capable of using them. Some of them, I doubt not, are excited to it by a sincere desire to know the Will of God, and what they shall do to be saved. Others, I am afraid, are actuated by the mean principles of curiosity, ambition, and vanity. However, be the principle what it will, I cannot but rejoice in the effect; as it renders them more capable of Instruction, in the great concerns of Religion.

Davies accepted motives of self-improvement only for spiritual ends.

The Hanover pastor insisted that the slaveowner not neglect the spiritual welfare of his chattels, "as though immorality were not a privilege common to them with their masters." But Samuel Davies himself owned slaves, and his concern did not extend far beyond their spiritual welfare. He insisted on humane treatment for slaves because the master had the same obligation to his Negroes as to his children. The one circumstance in which he told Negroes "it would be more tolerable . . . if you had still continued wild heathens in the deserts of Africa" involved baptism without a sincere religious belief. On the whole, Davies felt that the Negro was better off as a slave in America than free in Africa, since in the colonies he was exposed to the possibilities of salvation. Like most moderate New Lights, Davies was interested in missionary activity among the "Indian *Savages.*" Again, education for spiritual purposes was the basic motivation.

While the Awakening may have provided spiritual solace and improved treatment for Negroes and Indians, it did not produce any voices demanding fundamental alterations in their relationship to white society. Urgings for abolition of the slave trade, emancipation of the Negro, and a better deal for Indians continued to be faintly heard from moralists and those (like the Quakers) who remained completely outside the revival. When Isaac Backus preached a sermon titled *The Bondage of the Slave Woman and the Free,* the chains he had in mind were those of worldly security rather than chattel ownership. A generation after 1740, Samuel Hopkins of Newport would find some moral arguments in pietism against Negro slavery. But it is difficult to connect these events directly with the Great Awakening.

Sense of Community

Despite declining spiritual commitment, religious community, and traditional morality in the years before the Awakening, religion served as one of the major unifying and integrating aspects of life in colonial America. Only the church could provide a common value system (whatever its failures), and in most areas only the church could be a common meeting ground. The potentiality of the church was argued most strongly in those colonies where some form of established church was supported by public taxation or special state preference. Most clergy and many laymen felt the need for reinvigoration, and the Great Awakening, in its formative phases, was viewed by many as God's answer to existing weaknesses. The ultimate result of the revival for the community was mixed, however. In some areas, particularly on the frontier, it united and integrated a community. In others it united segments of the community while fragmenting the larger whole. In others still, revival simply fragmented.

The unifying and integrating force of the revival was largely a product of reinvigorated commitment. Integration was most obviously in places where the Awakening made possible the introduction of formal religion and the creation of a community church. But in other areas, where the community church had become weakened, the revival could also unite. In most cases it did so by dividing and forcing regrouping. Those who had experienced the ecstacy of conversion may have fought with those who had not, but if the result was two vigorous churches where previously there had been a single, quiescent one, this in some ways represented a gain for the community and its members. At least the Old Lights and New Lights cared, and found in their churches meaningful extensions of their own principles.

But the acrimonious debates associated with the revival were also forces of fragmentation. At the same time that responses to the Awakening bound segments of the population together in common religious experiences, values, and institutions, it also divided communities that previously had been united by a single church. Now there were churches and ministers that disagreed over public matters, and competed for public support. The debates could divide villages, neighborhoods, and even families.

Nevertheless, the importance of the revival in destroying a sense of community in colonial America must not be overemphasized. Many fragmenting factors had long been at work in the colonies, and the Awakening was frequently only a catalyst for existing forces. Local personality conflicts, disagreements over public policy, and economic disputes all played their part in setting New Light against Old Light. The revival fused more divisive elements than it created, and it frequently helped resolve conflict by creating more responsive ecclesiastical institutions which did not attempt to serve the entire local population. A larger, perhaps increasingly unrealistic sense of total community was lost at the same time that a more limited sense of community was gained. In any event, a close relationship between the church and the secular geopolitical unit was frequently altered by the revival.

One of the principal forces of community fragmentation was inherent in the growth of population and the expansion of settlement in colonial America. In settled regions, a growing population tended to escape the higher land prices of established communities by moving into the surrounding countryside. By the end of the seventeenth century, this movement was accompanied by a marked tendency to break with the Old World traditions of nucleated villages and open fields. Most Americans preferred to live on their farm lots, however much scattering of population resulted. Even in the relatively densely populated rural areas of New England, therefore, the inhabitants were well spread out.

By the beginning of the eighteenth century almost every town in coastal New England had a long-established church and other community facilities in an old portion of town, with its population increasing (and desirous of its own facilities, including churches) in outlying areas. The creation of new political units and new churches at the local level never kept pace with the expansion of settlement. At any point in time, a substantial and frequently vocal population considered itself badly served politically and ecclesiastically. The older community frequently fought desperately to keep its outlying population, since to lose it would result in higher per capita taxes and costs.

A population surge in the years immediately before 1740, just as the revival began, made the problem of convenient worship substantial and potentially ugly. In 1738, for example, a Cape Cod pastor had attempted to answer the complaint that "some People are remote from publick Worship, nor are able to maintain a suitably qualified Ministry," by arguing that "it can't be expected in scattering Towns, that all should have the publick Worship at or near their own Doors." This was hardly a satisfactory answer, especially after the revival had begun providing people with options.

The importance of local government was another factor of potential fragmentation. For most colonials, their immediate local government was the one which most directly affected them and the one with which they were most concerned. In the running of local churches, as in the running of secular government, the question was who should do the governing. Despite the pretensions of the ministry to dominate its congregations, by the time of the Great Awakening the dominance of the layman in governing the colonial churches was almost a universal fact. But, within lay dominance, which laymen? In every region, those who tended to dominate secular society also tended to control the churches. Urban churches frequently were run by merchants; churches in the plantation South were dominated by self-perpetuating oligarchies of planters who were organized into vestries; churches in rural farming and frontier communities were frequently governed by large bodies of farmers and artisans. But even in relatively open New England the "better sort" tended to run the churches, and in many cases these people came from the older, more established community.

The pressures upon clergymen who sought to maintain a position of authority were, understandably, considerable. The laymen with whom they struggled for dominance were frequently not the most pious people in the community; those in the outskirts, pleading for convenient worship, seemed more concerned about religion. Convinced that a truly Christian people would honor and obey their pastor, ministers were tempted not only to seek revival but to ally themselves with the new converts. Since areas that were badly served by traditional religion provided large pools of people who previously had been unaffected spiritually but were highly susceptible to evangelicalism, it was on the fringes of older communities where the Awakening frequently made its greatest impact. Revival thus increased the pressure for convenient and accessible places of worship on the part of a population whose recent and powerful religious experiences made them less likely to accept compromise. Many pastors thus found themselves caught between conflicting geographical sections of the community, which also had different religious experiences and aspirations.

However tempting alliance with new converts may have been for many ministers, particularly those who had fostered and supported revivalism, most settled clergymen ended up remaining with their older congregations. All too frequently the new converts—often combining years of religious deprivation and second-class ecclesiastical status with the logic of the "new birth"—pressed a position which, however consistent, was far too extreme for ministers to accept. Not in all cases did geographical and political conflict unite the pietists, but such a combination was fairly common, particularly in New England.

The experiences of Norwich, Connecticut, were not untypical. A large town in terms of area, Norwich had not yet finished the process of subdividing for ecclesiastical purposes when the Awakening occurred. The revival was supported chiefly by the pastor of the oldest Norwich church, Benjamin Lord. By 1745, Lord's church was under pressure from a number of new converts to exclude many of his older members who had not experienced crisis conversions. The critics also attacked other traditional practices of the church, including the halfway covenant. Many of the radicals came from a part of Lord's parish which they claimed to be

> so scituate as to Render . . . Attendance on the Publick Worship of God . . . exceeding Difficult, som of us Living more than six miles Distant from our Respective Places of Publick worship and the ordinary badness of the way together with the Extraordinary Difficulties of the winter and spring seasons Renders it impractical for us with our families many of which are numerous to attend on Divine worship as we would Gladly do.

Unable to alter church practices, the extremists withdrew from Lord's church and organized a Separate church closer to home. They ordained to the pastorate one of their number, who lacked formal education but felt the call to preach. The construction of a new meeting house for Lord's congregation which was even more inaccessible to the ill-served section, increased attendance at the Separate church, where the minister was supported by voluntary contributions.

"Separate" churches appeared all over New England in the 1740s, organized on the basis of an immediate relationship with God, objection to a classically educated "hireling Ministry" and ecclesiastical taxation, and rejection of all ecclesiastical compromise (increasingly including infant baptism). Many of these churches were supported by localities whose scattered population and relative penury made the new principles very practical. By

1750, nearly 100 Separate churches, most of them ephemeral, had been organized in New England. Many of them soon shifted to Baptist principles.

Although the Baptists were the chief beneficiaries of the division of the Awakening in New England, they were not the only denomination which made gains in the Northeast. In some areas where the Anglican church had gained a foothold, many of those who were repelled by the enthusiasm of the revival went over to the Church of England. Large towns and the area of southwestern Connecticut adjacent to New York City were the principal areas for Anglican expansion.

Outside New England, the Awakening contributed to the advancement of many denominations. In the Middle Colonies, many new converts—particularly those with Reformed or Lutheran backgrounds—joined one of the pietistic German sects whose principles were consistent with evangelicalism. The Moravian brotherhood, led by Count Zinzendorf, grew very rapidly. In the South, particularly in coastal Virginia, evangelical Presbyterianism became strong enough to challenge the Anglican ecclesiastical monopoly.

In all regions, the growth of new denominations was accompanied by divisions in the previously dominant groups. In most cases the issues went far beyond the simple approval or rejection of evangelicalism, however much that served as an ostensible basis of debate. Even the conservative Anglican church ultimately developed an evangelical wing, influenced partly by Wesleyan Methodism and partly by the loss of membership to pietistic denominations. The result of the growth of new denominations and division within existing ones was a new multiplicity of churches within a community. Colonials, particularly in rural districts, no longer had the limited choice of joining the community church or remaining outside it. Churches with a variety of beliefs and principles now competed openly. Membership in the community church, whether Anglican, Congregational, Presbyterian, or Reformed, carried different connotations after 1740. After the Great Awakening, community values could be associated with a community church only with difficulty, even when that church continued to be publicly supported.

Politics

Specific results of the Great Awakening have always been difficult to identify, and politics has been a particularly amorphous area. Most colonies in America had made some sort of accommodation to religious pluralism before 1740. Only Connecticut, which attempted to use the state to enforce ecclesiastical uniformity, developed a serious political division in which Old Lights and New Lights openly opposed one another in the legislative arena. Most of the divisions in most colonies occurred on the local level —complicated by other indigenous issues—and did not produce political alignments beyond the community. The merging of local questions into the debate over the Awakening made it difficult to find common denominators for political action over a broad geographical front. The revival *did* challenge potentially disruptive forces in the community, particularly the young, with spiritual concerns. This may have been a significant negative effect, but it did not produce anything positive in a political sense.

Nevertheless, one issue that was important to all was raised by the Great Awakening: religious toleration in those colonies maintaining established churches. Since most colonies in America —except Pennsylvania and Rhode Island—had some form of church establishment, most colonials had a stake in the issue. The question was most strenuously fought in Connecticut, which in 1742 attempted not only to protect the monopoly of its public churches with an "Act for Regulating Abuses and Correcting Disorders in Ecclesiastical Affairs" but declared open war on itinerancy, one of the basic principles of evangelical pietism. The act was directed principally against James Davenport and his supporters, but it was opposed by many moderate New Lights and by some Old Lights as well, who feared the principle of granting the state the power to punish ecclesiastical disorders. Many were concerned, as well, about the potential dangers to the colony's charter that were inherent in "restraining by penal law . . . liberty of conscience."

Throughout the mid-1740s, Connecticut extended its control over ecclesiastical affairs and vigorously prosecuted those who disregarded the 1742 act. Particularly hard hit were the Separates, who refused to pay taxes for the support of the standing churches, and whose very principles defied the laws. Many Separates, imprisoned for a variety of ecclesiastical and "civil" offenses, wrote pamphlets and petitions to the legislature and to the London Parliament demanding toleration. By 1750 Congregationalism felt the need for unity in the face of threats from Anglicans and Separates, and the laws of the 1740s were repealed. The repeal failed to relieve ecclesiastical disabilities on the local level, however, and the Separates fought on for full toleration.

Although Massachusetts did not attempt to invoke provincial legislation to deal with the disorders of the Awakening, as had Connecticut, it too put local dissenters at a disadvantage. The colony permitted taxes to be collected for the Congregational churches from all inhabitants except members of certain dissenting groups—Quakers, Anglicans, Baptists—which required complicated certification of their membership.

The movement for religious toleration in Massachusetts—and in New England generally—came to be led by the Middleborough Baptist pastor, Isaac Backus. Its principal thrust was to gain religious exemption from taxation on the local level for Separates and Baptists, but its limited success before the American Revolution led to a number of writings defending the concept of religious liberty many years after the revival. Particularly crucial here were Backus's *Appeal to the Public for Religious Liberty Against the Oppressions of the Present Day* (1773) and his *History of New England with Particular Reference to the Denomination Called Baptists* (the first volume of which was published in 1777). The *History* was a careful indictment of the religious persecutions of the Puritans and made a hero out of Roger Williams. The writings of Backus were a constant source of dismay to New England's revolutionary leaders, for the Baptist leader insisted on gaining the same rights and liberties for his denomination others were demanding from England. In 1774 Backus went to the Continental Congress to plead for religious liberty in New England—to the delight of the opponents of rebellion and the embarrassment of Puritan revolutionaries like Sam and John Adams.

In Virginia, the movement for toleration for dissenters was led by the Presbyterian minister Samuel Davies. On a visit to England in 1753/54, Davies got an opinion from the Attorney General that the English Toleration Act of 1689 (and subsequent supplementary legislation) applied fully to the dissenters in Virginia. Prior to 1755, when Virginia accepted the ruling, the Anglican authorities and the government in Virginia had attempted to license Presbyterians and thus control the activities of the denomination. A particular issue was the construction of many houses of worship to be served in circuit by a single minister. The Attorney General decided that Virginia had "no right to limit the number of houses for public worship to be allowed Dissenters" and "no right to specify the persons to speak in particular meetinghouses." After 1755, Britain's legal opinion and the threat of war in Virginia produced relative toleration for dissenters, especially the Presbyterians.

Although a few radical extremists, particularly within New England Separatism, argued for a complete separation of church and state, neither Backus nor Davies grounded their campaigns on such a principle. Both sought chiefly to remove disabilities against their own denominations, and both detested religious groups like the Quakers. Backus and Davies wanted little more than the extension to the colonies of the principles of religious toleration—hardly terribly radical—that had been won in England by the Revolution of 1688. Nevertheless, in their struggle for toleration both men were forced into the political arena, enlisting public support and petitioning legislatures and Parliament.

The battle for toleration (i.e., religious exemption) was the chief contact between the state and most pietists. Only when the practice of his religion was threatened did the typical pietist think at all in political terms. He was willing to "render unto Caesar" and wanted nothing more than to be left alone by the state. "Liberty of conscience" really meant "Leave me be." For the most part, dissenters had achieved religious freedom in practice, if not in principle, by the time of the American Revolution. The dismantling of state churches still remained in the future, and involved many factors besides the pietism unleashed by the Great Awakening, but the extension of toleration was the principal political achievement of the revival.

Despite the limited political impact of the Awakening, it has always been tempting to posit a relationship between the revival and the American movement for political independence, which began a generation later. However, twenty years added a good many new factors to the always shifting colonial situation. Many of those who were affected, or even molded, by the revival altered their views over time, and simple correlations do not work. The Congregational clergy, whose division over the Awakening was so general and bitter, reunited in the 1750s in the face of threats to their dominance from Separates and Anglicans. Thomas Clap, for example, president of Yale College and an opponent of revivalism in the 1740s, by the 1750s was leading a faction in Connecticut composed largely of men who had been the Awakening's supporters.

The Puritan clergy, so divided over the revival, were almost to a man united in support of the rebels. And many of the most radical pietists, like Isaac Backus, were at best hesitant revolutionaries. On the other hand, many Anglican clergymen, who ultimately backed the British became at least moderately sympathetic to Wesleyan evangelicalism—and Wesley himself was vehemently opposed to the Revolution—but Anglican laymen who had opposed evangelicalism formed the basis of the revolutionary movement in the South. Given such complications, establishing correlations between factions in the two movements is virtually impossible.

Even though correlations between individuals may be impossible, the contribution of the Awakening to the colonial climate of opinion is unmistakable. The evangelical pietism of the Great Awakening was clearly anti-authoritarian and basically individualistic. New Lights were forced by the ecclesiastical and political systems in which they lived to challenge the establishment. They did so out of moral fervor, convinced of its righteousness. The opponents of the revival were not inaccurate in their fears of the revolutionary potential implicit in the movement. Converts were encouraged, indeed required, to believe that their views were as valid as anyone's; they were, in the modern phrase, "true believers." In the 1740s this fervor was focused almost exclusively on ecclesiastical and spiritual matters because this was what revival was all about. After the decline of the Awakening in the coastal regions, pietism weakened to the point where it could be rechanneled into secular politics. Even in a somewhat less virulent strain, pietism was a faith which could sustain a revolution, and it may have done so for many.

The Great Awakening also played its part in breaking down sectional and parochial feelings in the colonies and in encouraging a new sense of American unity. War and external events had their effects as well. But the revival completely altered the denominational patterns of America. New England Congregationalism discovered its affinities with Middle Colony Presbyterianism, which was symbolized by the appointment of Jonathan Edwards to the presidency of the newly founded Presbyterian college at Princeton in 1756. New Light and Old Light wings of denominations in the various provinces reached out for contact and support to their compatriots in the other colonies. Presbyterians from the Middle Colonies and radical Congregationalists from New England moved into the Southern colonies in ever-increasing numbers. Itinerants like George Whitefield continued to travel about the colonies as though they were a single geographical unit.

The revival was not only America's first national experience but also its first mass movement. It introduced colonials to procedures and ways of action which well fitted a period of crisis. Few Americans considered the agitation and controversy of the years immediately before 1775 as a new departure in tactics or strategy; they had become standard procedure. Even fewer Americans analyzed the origins of the techniques they employed in opposing the British and fusing the thirteen colonies into a new nation. Had they done so, they would have traced them back to the Great Awakening.

The revival, while it had not introduced procedure, had conditioned men to accept certain activities as natural. When Bostonians gathered on Boston Common in 1773 to listen to an oration "on the Beauties of Liberty," the mass meeting they attended was a form that had been made respectable by George Whitefield in 1740. As Philadelphians, in newspapers and pamphlets, followed the complex intercolonial arguments over the nature of the Empire, a few may have recalled the many debates over the Awakening. For it was the revival which had first involved colonial Americans on a grand scale in confrontation politics, sloganeering, and ideological name-calling and labeling. The Great Awakening produced a general political polarization in matters of intellectual principle. Its great debates prefigured the great debates over the meaning of the Empire.

Epilogue

The Great Awakening never really ended; it moved from peak to peak of religious excitement. No other chronological period, however, equals in importance the first burst of enthusiasm. Ideas and techniques were then developed which would serve revivalism for over a century. By 1745, nevertheless, the rush for new church members had declined and the inevitable disillusionment of sustained controversy had set in. The second preaching tour of George Whitefield in 1745 was not met with public enthusiasm, and even the controversy was forced and tired. Thus 1745 is a convenient date, accepted by most contemporaries, for the termination of the first broad wave of religious excitement.

In fundamental ways, the first Great Awakening

remade American Protestantism, stamping it into patterns that remain familiar today. With its emphasis on immediate, individual experience, the revival brought New World Protestantism into harmony with many major intellectual currents of the time. Perhaps more significantly, an emphasis on immediate personal experience lessened the need for intellectual systems. In a large measure, experiential religion helped separate man's spiritual concerns from his intellectual life. In the nineteenth century the separation would become more distinct.

The intellectual climate of the eighteenth century, with its emphasis on the laws and order of nature, had removed God's immediate presence from man's religious life. Colonial theologians had struggled with the problem of restoring an ever-present and immediately active God Who functions outside the predictable system. The Great Awakening provided such a God by rejecting much of theology and focusing instead on the personal problem of salvation through conversion. The imperative presence of a free and mysterious God was part of the religious community's singularly simplistic focus in the eighteenth century. It aided in the separation of spiritual experience from ideas.

The search for salvation, when led by an evangelist, proved to be both highly emotional and largely unstructured. The Great Awakening, true to its Protestant roots, laid special and enduring emphasis on individual responsibility for conduct and personal rapport with God. The ultimate course to salvation seemed to rest with individual personalities, drawing into question both the need for church membership and the role of organized religion in the quest for personal fulfillment. As a result, American Protestantism would never again be as dependent upon a carefully structured hierarchical leadership as it had been in the seventeenth century. Protestantism in the New World would be marked by enormous denominational diversity and little regard for complex intellectual systems (commonly called theology).

Following the example of the Awakening, every independent spirit in America could see his particular or private religious experience as an unequivocal and inalienable truth. When this attitude was combined with some organizational talent or promotional interest, a new sect—and in some cases a new denomination—would emerge from the restraints of traditional religious forms and formulas. Inevitably, the religious diversity fostered by the revival created intense competition among the various religious interests for the minds and spirits of the people.

Those groups that were able to influence education, and particularly those that were capable of supplying trained clergy, had an important competitive advantage. Recognizing this point, revivalists became associated with the founding of new colleges, most notably Rhode Island College (later Brown University), Dartmouth College, and the College of New Jersey (later Princeton). These new seminaries, however, were only indirectly a product of the revival. Princeton supplied a long-felt need of the Presbyterians for a New World college, and revivalist energy provided some of the immediate impetus.

Significantly, involvement with the institutional structure of academic life tended to moderate the views of many revivalists and it restrained their independence. But a simplistic biblical outline, free of theological subtleties and independent of intellectual trends, became a distinguishing characteristic of new Protestant sects in America. Large segments of the Protestant community felt no need for special education as a prerequisite for mounting a pulpit. Anyone who attained the general educational level of his community and showed traits of character describable as wisdom could claim a pastorate. Thus the demands placed upon the clergy by the simplistic forms of the Great Awakening could be met by men of little academic pretension.

Moreover, the revival's emphasis on the clear distinction between saved and unsaved became part of a strong American ethical conviction. The distinction between good and bad was equally simple and free of subtlety—and even American foreign policy has been heir to this tradition. When the President of the United States surveys the international situation and distinguishes between good nations and bad nations, part of his public appeal is to an American belief that the United States has been "saved."

But if American manifest destiny and cold war politics have overtones of pietism, so do the underlying assumptions of many critics. We have seen a resurgence of individual concern for the soul among the young, reacting in large measure to the anxieties, formalisms, and complexities of modern life. This contemporary movement—including the use of drugs to generate a "mystical" personal experience—is less an heir to the tradition of the Great Awakening than a modern-form replication of the urges that produced it.

Bibliography

General Works on the Great Awakening

The most useful general account of the colonial Awakening is still *The Great Awakening: A History of the Revival of Religion in the Time of Edwards and Whitefield* by Joseph Tracy (Boston, 1841). A number of regional studies of more recent vintage are Edwin S. Gaustad, *The Great Awakening in New England* (New York, 1957); Charles H. Maxson, *The Great Awakening in the Middle Colonies* (Chicago, 1920); and Wesley M. Gewehr, *The Great Awakening in Virginia, 1740–1790* (Durham, N.C., 1930). One attempt to place the revival in the larger context of eighteenth-century colonial America is Cedric B.

Cowing's *The Great Awakening and the American Revolution: Colonial Thought in the 18th Century* (Chicago, 1971).

A number of collections of contemporary documents have been published within the past few years: Alan Heimert and Perry Miller (eds.), *The Great Awakening: Documents Illustrating the Crisis and Its Consequences* (Indianapolis and New York, 1967); David S. Lovejoy (ed.), *Religious Enthusiasm and the Great Awakening* (Englewood Cliffs, N.J., 1969); Richard L. Bushman (ed.), *The Great Awakening: Documents on the Revival of Religion, 1740–1745* (New York, 1970); and J. M. Bumsted (ed.), *The Great Awakening: The Beginnings of Evangelical Pietism in America* (Waltham, Mass., 1970). Darrett B. Rutman (ed.), *The Great Awakening: Event and Exegesis* (New York, 1970), contains historical documents and selections from important modern interpretive essays.

The Religious Background

For New England, consult Ola Winslow, *Meetinghouse Hill, 1630–1783* (New York, 1952); Clifford K. Shipton, "The New England Clergy of the 'Glacial Age'," *Proceedings of the Colonial Society of Massachusetts,* XXXII (1933), 24–54; H. B. Parkes, "New England in the Seventeen-Thirties," *New England Quarterly,* III (1930), 397–419; and J. M. Bumsted, "A Caution to Erring Christians: Ecclesiastical Disorder on Cape Cod, 1717–1738," *William and Mary Quarterly,* XXVIII (1971), 413–438.

For Presbyterianism, especially in the Middle Colonies, see Leonard J. Trinterud, *The Forming of an American Tradition: A Re-Examination of Colonial Presbyterianism* (Philadelphia, 1949). The Dutch church is examined in James Tanis, *Dutch Calvinistic Pietism in the Middle Colonies: A Study of the Life and Theology of Theodorus Jacobus Frelinghuysen* (The Hague, 1968). For the Anglicans, see George M. Brydon, *Virginia's Mother Church and the Political Conditions under Which It Grew: The Story of the Anglican Church and the Development of Religion in Virginia; 1727–1814* (Philadelphia, 1952).

A recent and general bibliography of works on the colonial period has been collected in Jack P. Greene (ed.), *The American Colonies in the Eighteenth Century, 1689-1763* (New York, 1969).

Communities and Tensions

The standard works on American cities in the colonial period are Carl Bridenbaugh's *Cities in the Wilderness: The First Century of Urban Life in America, 1625–1742* (New York, 1938) and *Cities in Revolt: Urban Life in America, 1743–1776* (New York, 1955). A recent and important study of a single city is G. B. Warden's *Boston, 1689–1776* (Boston, 1970). See also Warden's "L'urbanisation Américaine avant 1800," a review article in *Annales Economies Sociétés Civilisations* (25 année, 1970), pp. 862–879.

For the settled agrarian community, consult Philip Greven, *Four Generations: Population, Land and Family in Colonial Andover, Massachusetts* (Ithaca, N.Y., 1970); Kenneth Lockridge, *A New England Town: The First Hundred Years* (New York, 1970); Michael Zuckerman, *Peaceable Kingdoms: New England Towns in the Eighteenth Century* (New York, 1970); James T. Lemon, *The Best Poor Man's Country: A Geographical Study of Early Southeastern Pennsylvania* (Baltimore, 1971); and Douglas Southall Freeman, *Young Washington: A Selection from the Biography* (New York, 1966).

For child-rearing practices, see John Demos, *A Little Commonwealth: Family Life in Plymouth Colony* (New York, 1970), and two works by Edmund S. Morgan: *The Puritan Family: Religion and Domestic Relations in Seventeenth Century New England* (New York, 1966) and *Virginians at Home: Family Life in the Eighteenth Century* (Williamsburg, Va., 1952). For education generally, see Bernard Bailyn, *Education in the Forming of American Society: Needs and Opportunities for Study* (Chapel Hill, N.C., 1960).

For back-country settlements, see Douglas E. Leach, *The Northern Colonial Frontier, 1607–1763* (New York, 1966); Robert Ramsey, *Carolina Cradle: Settlement of the Northwest Carolina Frontier, 1747–1762* (Chapel Hill, 1964); Charles E. Clark, *The Eastern Frontier: The Settlement of Northern New England, 1610–1763* (New York, 1970); and Charles S. Grant, *Democracy in the Connecticut Frontier Town of Kent* (New York, 1961).

Colonial tensions and the impact of war are discussed in Howard H. Peckham, *The Colonial Wars, 1689–1762* (Chicago, 1964). A general discussion of tensions in one important colony is provided in Richard L. Bushman, *From Puritan to Yankee: Character and the Social Order in Connecticut, 1690–1765* (Cambridge, Mass., 1967).

For economic difficulties, see E. James Ferguson, "Currency Finance: An Interpretation of Colonial Monetary Practices," *William and Mary Quarterly,* X (1953), 153–180, and Theodore G. Thayer, "The Land-Bank System in the American Colonies, " *Journal of Economic History,* XIII (1953), 145–159.

For epidemics, consult John Duffy, *Epidemics in Colonial America* (Baton Rouge, 1953), and Ernest Caulfield, *A True History of the Terrible Epidemic Vulgarly Called the Throat Distemper Which Occurred in His Majesty's New England Colonies Between the Years 1735 and 1740* (New Haven, 1939).

For violence and insurrections, see Herbert Aptheker, *American Negro Slave Revolts* (New York, 1943), and Ferenc M. Szasz, "The New York Slave Revolt of 1741: A Re-examination, " *New York History,* XLVIII (1967), 215–230.

The European Background

Two works supply perceptive insight into the intellectual climate of the eighteenth century: Richard Foster Jones, *Ancients and Moderns: A Study in the Background of the Battle of the Books* (St. Louis, 1961), and Basil Willey, *The 18th Century Background: Studies on the Idea of Nature in the Thought of the Period* (New York, 1941).

For specific attention to the religious background, a recent and sensitive account is Charles H. And Katherine George, *The Protestant Mind of the English Reformation* (Princeton, 1961). And William Haller's *The Rise of Puritanism* (New York, 1938) is still invaluable.

For the relationship between Puritanism and the "new science," see the account of the long historiographical dispute in Richard L. Greaves, "Puritanism and Science: The Anatomy of a Controversy," *Journal of the History of Ideas,* XXX (1969), 345–368. See, too, John Dillenberger, *Protestant Thought and Natural Science* (New York, 1960).

For an examination of the systematic origins of Puritanism, against which the revival in part revolted, see Keith L. Spranger, "Technometria: A Prologue to Puritan Theology," *Journal of the History of Ideas*, XXIX (1968), 115–122. Although there is little literature available in English dealing with the Continental pietists, see the early chapters of Tanis, *Dutch Calvinistic Pietism*, and John Preston Haskins, "German Influence on Religious Life and Thought in America during the Colonial Period, " *Princeton Theological Magazine*, V (1907), 49–79. For the English movement, W. K. Louther Clarke, *Eighteenth Century Piety* (London, 1944)—essentially a history of the Society for Providing Christian Knowledge—contains some useful information. More valuable is Eric W. Baker, *A Herald of the Evangelical Revival: A Critical Inquiry into the Relation of William Law to John Wesley and the Beginning of Methodism* (London, 1948). Additional background material can be found in Luke Tyerman, *Life and Times of . . . John Wesley*, 3 vols. (London, 1872–1875), and Stuart C. Henry, *George Whitefield: Wayfaring Witness* (Nashville, 1957).

The American Background

The literature for understanding the American Puritans is voluminous. Everyone who deals with the topic should know the works of Perry Miller, for he set the tone for a generation of scholarship. See especially Miller's *The New England Mind: The Seventeenth Century* (Cambridge, Mass., 1939) and *The New England Mind: From Colony to Province* (Cambridge, Mass., 1953). For Miller's special place in Puritan historiography and as particular background for the Great Awakening, consult George M. Marsden, "Perry Miller's Rehabilitation of the Puritans: A Critique," *Church History*, XXXIX (1970), 91–105. Additional background can be found in Gerald J. Goodwin, "The Myth of 'Arminian-Calvinism' in Eighteenth Century New England," *New England Quarterly*, XLI (1968), 213–237; Cynthia Griffin Wolff, "Literary Reflections of the Puritan Character," *Journal of the History of Ideas*, XXIX (1968), 13–32; and Leonard T. Grant, "Puritan Catechizing," *Journal of Presbyterian History*, XLVI (1968), 107–127.

John E. Van de Wetering, "God, Science and the Puritan Dilemma," *New England Quarterly*, XXXVIII (1965), 494–507, discusses the impact of the "new science."

The basic documents of American Puritanism are available in Williston Walker, *The Creeds and Platforms of Congregationalism* (New York, 1893, and Boston, 1969). Although more than a decade old, Nelson R. Burr, *A Critical Bibliography of Religion in America*, 2 vols. (Princeton, 1961), is still useful.

For the mood in New England that led to revival, see especially Cotton Mather, *Bonifacius, An Essay Upon the Good,* ed. David Levin (Cambridge, Mass., 1966), and Robert Middlekauff, *The Mathers: Three Generations of Puritan Intellectuals, 1596–1728* (New York, 1971). For a special view of Mather and Francke, see Ernest Benz, "Pietist and Puritan Sources of Early Protestant World Mission," *Church History,* XX (1951), 28–39.

The Course of The Awakening

George Whitefield's accounts of his tour have been collected in *George Whitefield's Journals* (London, 1960). The best biographies are Luke Tyerman, *The Life of the Rev. George Whitefield* (London, 1877), and Stuart C. Henry, *George Whitefield: Wayfaring Witness*. A recent article that emphasizes Whitefield's urban success is William Howland Kenney 3d, "George Whitefield, Dissenter Priest of the Great Awakening, 1739–1741," *William and Mary Quarterly*, XXVI (1969), 75–93. For Whitefield and Garden, see Kenney's "Alexander Garden and George Whitefield: The Significance of Revivalism in South Carolina, 1738–1741," *South Carolina Historical Magazine,* LXXI (1970), 1–16.

For the psychology of conversion, see Elmer T. Clark, *The Psychology of Religious Awakening* (New York, 1929), and William Sargant, *The Battle for the Mind* (New York, 1957). The general secondary studies and documentary collections cited earlier all contain accounts of the extension of the revival in rural areas. See also J. M. Bumsted, "Revivalism and Separatism in New England: The First Society of Norwich, Connecticut, as a Case Study," *William and Mary Quarterly*, XXIV (1967), 588–612.

For New Hampshire, consult Clark's *The Eastern Frontier,* pp.

272th ff. For an Anglican evaluation of the revival in New England, see Douglas C. Stenerson, "An Anglican Critique of the Early Phase of the Great Awakening in New England: A Letter by Timothy Cutler," *William and Mary Quarterly*, XXX (1973), 475–488.

There is no definitive biography of Charles Chauncy, but see Harold E. Bernhard, *Charles Chauncy: Colonial Liberal, 1705–1787* (Chicago, 1948), and B. L. Jones, "Charles Chauncy and the Great Awakening in New England," unpublished Ph.D. dissertation, Duke University (1958).

For the Connecticut repressions, consult Bushman, *From Puritan to Yankee*; C. C. Goen, *Revivalism and Separatism in New England: Strict Congregationalists and Separate Baptists in the Great Awakening* (New Haven, 1962); and William G. McLoughlin, *New England Dissent, 1630–1833: The Baptists and the Separation of Church and State*, 2 vols. (Cambridge, Mass., 1971), which is also the best source for the radical New Lights. But see also McLouglin's *Isaac Backus and the American Pietistic Tradition* (Boston, 1967) and Dietmar Rothermund, *The Layman's Progress: Religious and Political Experience in Colonial Pennsylvania, 1740–1770* (Philadelphia, 1962).

For the Southern phase of the revival, see David T. Morgan, "The Great Awakening in North Carolina, 1740–1755: The Baptist Phase," *North Carolina Historical Review*, XXXXV (1968), 264—283; George William Pilcher, *Samuel Davies: Apostle of Dissent in Colonial Virginia* (Knoxville, 1971); Robert Sutherland Alley, "The Reverend Mr. Samuel Davies: A Study in Religion and Politics, 1747–1759," unpublished Ph.D. dissertation, Princeton University (1962); and Rhys Isaac, "Religion and Authority: Problems of the Anglican Establishment in Virginia in the Era of the Great Awakening and the Parsons' Cause," *William and Mary Quarterly*, XXX (1973), 3–36.

For Nova Scotia, consult M. W. Armstrong, *The Great Awakening in Nova Scotia, 1776–1809* (Hartford, 1948); J. M. Bumsted, *Henry Alline, 1748–1784* (Toronto, 1971); and Gordon Stewart and George Rawlyk, *A People Highly Favoured of God: The Nova Scotia Yankees and the American Revolution* (Toronto, 1972).

The Factions of the Awakening

For an examination of the moderates' receptivity to revival, especially in New England, see Norman Pettit, *The Heart Prepared: Grace and Conversion in Puritan Spiritual Life* (New Haven, 1966); C. J. Sommerville, "Conversion versus the Early Puritan Covenant of Grace," *Journal of Presbyterian History*, XLIV (1966), 178–197; and Harold M. Feinstein, "The Prepared Heart: A Comparative Study of Puritan Theology and Psychoanalysis," *American Quarterly*, XXII (1970), 166–176.

A basic source of information on the particular events of revival is Thomas Prince Jr., *The "Christian History"* (Boston, 1744—1745). For an analysis of this basic source, see John E. Van de Wetering, "The 'Christian History' of the Great Awakening," *Journal of Presbyterian History*, XLIV (1966), 122–129.

A great deal of general information on the moderates is available in Gaustad, *The Great Awakening in New England*. Trinterud's *Forming of an American Tradition* is especially valuable for understanding Jonathan Dickinson and the Middle Colony moderates.

The literature on Jonathan Edwards is voluminous. The collected works are readily available as *The Works of President Edwards: A Reprint of the Worcester Edition*, 4 vols. (New York, 1854). A modern and scholarly edition of Edwards' writing is being published *seriatum* by Yale University. For a selective bibliography of older writings on Edwards, see Burr, *A Critical Bibliography*.

Important articles appropriate to this study include Perry Miller, "Jonathan Edwards on the Sense of the Heart," *Harvard Theological Review*, XLI (1948), 123–145; Paul Hehn, "John Locke and Jonathan Edwards: A Reconsideration," *Journal of the History of Philosophy*, VII (1969), 51–61; Edward H. Davidson, "From Locke to Edwards," *Journal of the History of Ideas*, XXIV (1963), 355–372; and David C. Pierce, "Jonathan Edwards and the 'New Sense' of Glory," *New England Quarterly*, XLI (1968), 82–95. See also Edward H. Davidson, *Jonathan Edwards: The Narrative of a Puritan Mind* (Cambridge, Mass., 1968), and Douglas J. Elwood,

The Philosophical Theology of Jonathan Edwards (New York, 1960).

There is very little recent secondary material for those characteristics described here as radical. For biographical sketches of the figures mentioned, see John Langdon Sibley and Clifford K. Shipton (eds.), *Biographical Sketches of Graduates of Harvard College*, 14 vols. (Cambridge, Mass., 1873–1970), and Franklin B. Dexter (ed.), *Biographical Sketches of the Graduates of Yale College, 1701–1815*, 6 vols. (New Haven, 1885–1912). Trinterud's *The Forming of an American Tradition* has valuable material on the radical figures of the Middle Colonies, and McLoughlin's *New England Dissent* is useful for New England radicalism. See also Archibald Alexander, *Biographical Sketches of the Founder, and Principal Alumni of the Log College* (Princeton, 1845); K. Ludwig DeBenneville, "Memorabilia of the Tennents," *Journal of the Presbyterian Historical Society*, I (1902), 344–354; William T. Hanzsche, "New Jersey Moulders of the American Presbyterian Church," *Journal of the Presbyterian Historical Society*, XXI (1946), 71–82; and Thomas C. Pears Jr. and Guy S. Klett, "Documentary History of William Tennent and the Log College," *Journal of the Presbyterian Historical Society*, XXVIII (1950), 38–62.

For Davenport, the standard histories by Tracy and Gaustad are the most accessible published accounts; the best analysis is Lawrence N. Jones, "James Davenport, Prodigal of the Great Awakening," unpublished paper from the Yale Divinity School (1957).

For the Separates, see C. C. Goen, *Revivalism and Separatism*.

For the doctrine of assurance, see Arthur S. Yates, *The Doctrine of Assurance with Special Reference to John Wesley* (London, 1952).

Demographic Characteristics

Except for the two papers upon which the table of numbers in the text is based, there has been no analytical or extensive study of the demographic question. For demographic characteristics, see J. M. Bumsted, "Religion, Finance, and Democracy in Massachusetts: The Town of Norton as a Case Study," *Journal of American*

History, LVII (1971), 817–831, and Philip J. Greven Jr., "Youth, Maturity, and Religious Conversion: A Note on the Ages of Converts in Andover, Massachusetts, 1711–1749," *Essex Institute Historical Collections*, CVIII (1972), 119–134.

For the problem of sex ratio, see Cedric B. Cowing, "Sex and Preaching in the Great Awakening," *American Quarterly*, XX (1968), 624–644. No serious study of the effect of the Awakening on America's racial minorities has ever been undertaken.

For missionary work, see R. Pearce Beaver, "American Missionary Motivation before the Revolution," *Church History*, XXXI (1962), 216–226. For the impact of the revival on Southern Negroes, consult Joseph B. Earnest, *The Religious Development of the Negro in Virginia* (Charlottesville, 1914), and Mary F. Goodwin, "Christianizing and Educating the Negro in Colonial Virginia," *Historical Magazine of the Protestant Episcopal Church*, I (1932), 143–152.

The effects of revivalism in diffusing political revolution are discussed in M. W. Armstrong, "Neutrality and Religion in Revolutionary Nova Scotia," *New England Quarterly*, XIX (1946), 50–62, and Bumsted, *Henry Alline*, pp. 64ff.

Social Impact

On morality, consult C. F. Adams, "Some Phases of Sexual Morality and Church Discipline in Colonial New England," *Proceedings of the Massachusetts Historical Society*, VI (1891), 477–516; H. B. Parkes, "Sexual Morals in the Great Awakening," *New England Quarterly*, III (1930), 133–135; Emil Oberholzer, *Delinquent Saints: Disciplinary Action in the Early Congregational Churches of Massachusetts* (New York, 1956), especially the tables on pp. 252–260; and Richard J. Hooker (ed.), *The Carolina Backcountry on the Eve of the Revolution: The Journal and Other Writings of Charles Woodmason, Anglican Itinerant* (Chapel Hill, 1953). The quotations of confessions and relations are from the Freetown (Mass.) Church Records, Fall River Historical Society.

The "destruction" of communities is discussed implicitly in Goen, *Revivalism and Separatism*, and in McLoughlin, *New England Dissent*, and explicitly in Bushman, *From Puritan to Yankee*, and Rothermund, *Layman's Progress*. See also Bumsted, "Revivalism and Separatism in New England: The First Society of Norwich, Connecticut, as a Case Study," *William and Mary Quarterly*, XXIV (1967), 588–612, and "Presbyterianism in 18th Century Massachusetts: The Formation of a Church at Easton, 1752," *Journal of Presbyterian History*, XLVI (1968), 243–253. Also important is Timothy L. Smith, "Congregation, State, and Denomination: The Forming of the American Religious Structure," *William and Mary Quarterly*, XXV (1968), 155–176.

For the political impact of the revival in Connecticut, see Bushman and Robert Sklar, "The Great Awakening and Colonial Politics: Connecticut's Revolution in the Minds of Men," *Connecticut Historical Society Bulletin*, XXVII (1963), 87-95.

For toleration, consult William G. McLoughlin (ed.), *Isaac Backus on Church, State, and Calvinism: Pamphlets, 1754–1789* (Cambridge, Mass., 1968), as well as his "Isaac Backus and the Separation of Church and State in America," *American Historical Review*, LXXII (1968), 1392–1413, and his *New England Dissent*.

For Samuel Davies, see G. W. Pilcher, "Samuel Davies and Religious Toleration in Virginia," *The Historian*, XXVIII (1965), 48–71.

Alan Heimert's *Religion and the American Mind: From the Great Awakening to the Revolution* (Cambridge, Mass., 1966) is reviewed sympathetically by William G. McLoughlin in *New England Quarterly*, XL (1967), 99–110, and critically by Edmund S. Morgan in *William and Mary Quarterly*, XXIV (1967), 454–459. Morgan has stated his own position in "The Puritan Ethic and the American Revolution," *William and Mary Quarterly*, XXIV (1967), 3–43.

Index